What people are saying about

The Mongolian Death Worm: On the Hunt in the Gobi Desert

Pat Spain is that rare thing: a rationalist who still embraces the possible and knows that there are more things in heaven and earth than are dreamt of. A grown-up who has lost none of the childhood wonder and curiosity that makes the world magical. A scientist who keeps an open mind and rejoices in the fact that absence of proof is not proof of absence. There is nobody I'd want to travel with more to explore the wild side of our literally extraordinary planet. Buckle up and prepare for adventures.
Harry Marshall, Chairman and Co-Founder of Icon Films

Pat is a natural storyteller on screen, but this takes the stories we've seen to a whole new level. This is an incredibly immersive deep dive into the cultures and experiences of making a film that you won't be able to put down once you've started.
Rob Nelson, Biologist and Filmmaker

Other titles in the On the Hunt series

200,000 Snakes: On the Hunt in Manitoba
A Bulletproof Ground Sloth: On the Hunt in Brazil
A Little Bigfoot: On the Hunt in Sumatra
A Living Dinosaur: On the Hunt in West Africa
Sea Serpents: On the Hunt in British Columbia
The Mongolian Death Worm: On the Hunt in the Gobi Desert

T0027205

The Mongolian Death Worm: On the Hunt in the Gobi Desert

or How I Found the Worst Bathroom on Earth and Learned to Love Cheese Flavored Vodka

The Mongolian Death Worm: On the Hunt in the Gobi Desert

or How I Found the Worst Bathroom on Earth and Learned to Love Cheese Flavored Vodka

Pat Spain

6TH
BOOKS

Winchester, UK
Washington, USA

JOHN HUNT PUBLISHING

First published by Sixth Books, 2022
Sixth Books is an imprint of John Hunt Publishing Ltd., No. 3 East St., Alresford,
Hampshire SO24 9EE, UK
office@jhpbooks.com
www.johnhuntpublishing.com
www.6th-books.com

For distributor details and how to order please visit the 'Ordering' section on our website.

Text copyright: Pat Spain 2021

ISBN: 978 1 78904 650 2
978 1 78904 651 9 (ebook)
Library of Congress Control Number: 2021942240

A CIP catalogue record for this book is available from the British Library.

Design: Stuart Davies

UK: Printed and bound by CPI Group (UK) Ltd, Croydon, CR0 4YY
Printed in North America by CPI GPS partners

We operate a distinctive and ethical publishing philosophy in
all areas of our business, from our global network of authors to
production and worldwide distribution.

Contents

This book is for my wife Anna and our kids, Luna and Wally.
Let's go on an adventure, I'll bring snacks.

Introduction

Some of you may know me as "The (almost) King of the Jungle", "Legend Hunter", "That animal guy", "Beast Hunter" or "That guy who had cancer and catches snakes". Probably not, though; despite having a couple dozen hours of international TV series to my name, and giving hundreds of talks and presentations, I don't really get recognized very often – unless we are talking about college kids in Guwahati, India, middle-aged men in the US, or preteen Indonesian girls – my key demographics, it turns out. I struggle to name anything those groups have in common, besides me.

I left my home in Upstate New York at 16 to live in a barn in southern Maine for a marine biology internship, and I haven't stopped exploring since. My passion for wildlife led me to create my own YouTube-based wildlife series in 2004 and has landed me spots on Animal Planet, Nat Geo, Nat Geo Wild, Travel Channel, SyFy, BBC and more. Half of the TV shows I've made have never seen the light of day, but they were all an adventure and there isn't a single one I wouldn't do again if given the chance. Besides TV, I work full time in biotech, which is its own sort of adventure – albeit one where drinking the water is generally safer. I've been bitten and stung by just about everything you can think of – from rattlesnakes and black bears to bullet ants and a rabid raccoon, and I've lost count of the number of countries I've been to.

I've had the opportunity to travel the world interacting with some of the strangest and rarest animals while having the honor of living with indigenous peoples in some of the most remote locations – participating in their rituals, eating traditional meals, and massively embarrassing myself while always trying to remain respectful. I am a perpetual fish-out-of-water, even in my home state of Massachusetts. This book is part of the

"On the Hunt" series, in which I get to tell some of my favorite stories from those travels.

This particular book is about my time in Mongolia searching for the truth behind an animal whose name sounds like a metal band – the Mongolian Death Worm – with my friends, making an episode of the National Geographic Channel series *Beast Hunter*, also called *Beast Man* in the UK, *Breast Hunter* by my wife, and *Beast Master* by almost everyone who meets me for the first time and tells me they enjoyed the series.

Mongolia is amazing – the people, the sites, the wildlife. Aside from the bottom of the ocean, the Gobi Desert looks the most like an alien landscape of the places I've been. At times, it felt like Tatooine. I love and respect the land, the people, and the animals, and feel privileged to have been able to experience it for myself. There is some pretty inappropriate humor in here. Please take it for what it is – humor – and know that I mean no disrespect. I hope you enjoy this book. If you do, please pick up the others from this series. If you don't, I'll probably hear about why on social media. Either way, thanks for reading!

A disclaimer

My dog Daisy was the best. She loved hanging out in the backyard with my sister Sarah and me when we were playing hide-and-go-seek, catching bugs, or looking for arrowheads on the trails behind our house in Upstate NY. She would wait patiently at the base of any tree we climbed and chase away our neighbor's super scary dog (he ate a kitten once). She would also stand guard while I waited for the spider to crawl out of a crack in our chipped blue bulkhead cellar doors. It was huge, with green-metallic colored fur and red eyes, and Daisy would growl if I put my hand too close it. She was a white poodle mix with poofy fur and perpetually muddy feet. Also, Daisy could fly, sometimes wore a cape, and would occasionally speak with a Southern drawl.

I don't have schizophrenia and Daisy was not an imaginary friend – but she also didn't really exist. Despite never owning a dog as a child, I have honest, distinct memories of Daisy. Memories that go well beyond the stories my mom used to tell my sister and me about Daisy saving us from one tragedy or another. I also have detailed memories of being terrified, like heart-racing, nearly-in-tears fear the time Cookie Monster stole our shoes while we were wading in the creek catching crayfish and pollywogs. He would only give them back when we had the Count (who smelled like toothpaste) help us negotiate how many cookies it would take for each shoe, shoelace, and sock. Daisy ran back and forth from our house bringing with her a ransom of the ever-increasing number of chocolate chip cookies that my mom had left out to cool. The monster (I think people forget he is a monster by definition) kept finding loopholes in our deals, and the tension was getting higher and higher as the water rose in the creek. Cookie Monster smelled like BO and his eyes rolled around like a crazy person's. He was unstable. In the end, Daisy came through, as she always did.

Mom would start these stories, "When you were both very small, we had a wonderful dog named Daisy," and they quickly took on a life of their own. They eventually made their way into our collective consciousness as real events, complete with details not included in the original stories which must have been added by Sarah and me. It was years later, during some holiday involving drinking (see "every holiday"), that we started reminiscing about childhood memories and one of us asked: "Did we really have a dog when we were little? I kind of feel like we did, but I also can't picture us having a dog with all of the other animals we had. Daisy, maybe?" It wasn't until then that we realized these were, in fact, fictitious stories our mom had made up to keep us entertained on rainy days in our old house. Stories that drew on real events (being terrorized by a neighbor's dog, getting stuck in a creek, finding snakes, spiders, and arrowheads, etc.), with Daisy taking the place of our mother as the heroine.

I guess what I mean by this is, all of the stories in this book are exactly how I remember them, but I honestly remember having a flying southern-belle dog and interacting with Muppets. Take that how you want. I had a great childhood.

Oh, also – All views expressed are my own and do not reflect those of National Geographic, the National Geographic Channel, Icon Films, John Hunt Publishing, or any other person or organization mentioned (or not mentioned) in this book.

Chapter 1

Dance, Dance Now, Dance like an Eagle

The reality of the situation I found myself in didn't really sink in until I felt a cool breeze on my inner thighs. I was, in fact, really standing there, wearing bikini briefs, upturned, pointy-toed, fancy boots, a bedazzled off-the-shoulder shrug, and a very phallic-looking hat, about to wrestle a giant Mongolian man in front of hundreds of nomads, in the middle of the Gobi Desert – a debacle that was being filmed for international television. Having quickly come to terms with that fact, my next thought was, "If I move my leg even slightly too high, this episode is going to be NC-17."

I was three days in on a shoot for the TV series *Beast Hunter* – a National Geographic Channel production helmed by Icon Films searching for the truth behind some of the world's most persistent wildlife legends. This episode was about my hunt for an animal with the distinction of having the greatest name in all of cryptozoology – the Mongolian Death Worm – and we were already behind schedule. On day one, none of our luggage or film equipment had arrived from Moscow, and no one at the airport in Ulaanbaatar seemed surprised. In fact, they were very interested in why *we* were surprised. They told us that oversized luggage is always one day behind – in other words, yesterday's luggage arrives on today's flight, always. This was, in my opinion, an interesting way of doing business. The immediate issue was that we couldn't leave the sprawling Soviet Bloc-style capital of Mongolia for two nights. I wasn't complaining, as this meant I could enjoy an extra day of flushing toilets (although they smelled horrible – I really don't know how an indoor toilet could possibly manage to smell worse than a long drop in equatorial Africa, but here we were), showering (I was soon to break my previous record of eight nights without any water touching my body), and hotel food which included generic Laughing Cow rip-off cheese bits called Paprika Happy Cow, and featured a super-trippy image of a manic-looking cartoon cow that seemed to be in the midst of a mental breakdown on the front.

Without our gear there was very little productive work we could do, so we spent the day exploring possible filming locations, drinking, and getting to know our guide and fixer, Batzorig, a young Mongolian man to whom we would be trusting our lives for the next couple weeks. Batzorig (like many Mongolians) seemed to combine the best stereotypical physical attributes of his Russian and Chinese neighbors. He had a round face with a well-defined jawline and high cheekbones, was not large but solid and strong. Batzorig was good-humored, perpetually smiling, and though quick to laugh, could also be stern and serious. He always had a good story, loved his country and really enjoyed sharing it with us crazy Westerners. His accent was unique, but close to stereotypical Russian. The Mongolian language is very guttural and, in Batzorig's own words, "requires you to sound like you are coughing and hurting your throat" to properly pronounce anything. And he could *drink*. Vodka was, of course, the drink of choice, and we imbibed quite a bit. Chinggis was the most popular brand and led to a startling discovery – Genghis Khan, debatably the most famous Mongolian of all time, was not named Genghis Khan.

Batzorig explained that like so many Smythe's before him, Genghis Khan was the victim of name-Westernization. When Europeans recorded the history of Khan's conquests (a source of pride for many Mongolians to this day), they made a couple of clerical errors, turned the "C" into a "G", and turned "Chinggis" into "Genghis" and, according to Batzorig, "The Mongolian people were too polite to correct them."

"For centuries?" James, our sound technician, asked, stunned. James, the most positive person I've ever met, was the sound recordist for every episode of *Beast Hunter*. He is five years younger than me, exceptionally handsome, blonde-haired, blue-eyed, scruffy-bearded, incredibly bright, has been everywhere and seen everything, and is nearly always in a fantastic mood. Basically, everyone at Icon is amazing and some of the greatest, most talented people I've ever come across. But even among this group of superhumans, James is a standout. Not only is he talented in literally all aspects of production (he directs, produces, edits, writes, is a cameraman, sound recordist, drone operator, first responder, and general tech for all equipment), but he's an amazing guy and a great friend. He's hysterically funny – VERY inappropriate, but extremely respectful to every person he comes into contact with. He always asks for people's names, and actually listens and pays attention to whomever he is speaking with. His partner Jen is just as kind, talented, and wonderful, and they have two amazing girls who will probably never appreciate how lucky they are to have these two as their parents.

Batzorig replied, "Eh, it isn't that big a deal to us. We call him Chinggis, you call him Genghis. Who cares? He is still the same man." This was a small glimpse into the incredible kindness of the Mongolian people. For a culture often associated with an ancient warlord, it may surprise people to hear that the nomads we lived with were the most generous, inviting, and compassionate group of people I have ever had the pleasure of getting to know. There was a poorly translated Mongolian tourism magazine on the plane to this lovely country, and when describing the Mongolian people it said, "They have good hearts, but angry faces," and "None of them hate you as much as you think they do." I never thought any of the wonderful Mongolians we stayed with hated us, even a little.

Batzorig brought us to a giant outdoor market far outside

of town to purchase various trinkets. Our crew *loved* trinkets – the cheesier the better. We all had collections of bizarre statues, fridge magnets, "art", and other "tat", as the Brits call it. Batzorig tried in vain to teach me a few Mongolian words on the way. The word for the death-worm was particularly troubling and generally left my mouth with a sound similar to that which one might make while hacking up a fingernail lodged in the tonsils. As our 1970s' "luxury" minibus approached the market, my Mongolian little improved, the traffic came to a sudden stop. People were approaching from all directions in many different Soviet-era vehicles, goods-laden carts, and motorbikes. Batzorig explained that this was a popular weekend activity for families and people came from miles around to shop, eat, sell their stuff, and hang out at the mix of flea market, food court, produce bazaar, and antique dealer. He warned us that if we were going to get robbed in Mongolia, it would be here. Pickpockets were the main scourge of the market.

We parked and Laura, our associate producer, handed out our Mongolian money – about 45,000 tugriks each, or $25 US. She had converted it for us in the backroom of a shady bodega earlier in the day on Batzorig's recommendation. He said she would get the best exchange rate here because he "knew the guy". He parked in a back alley and insisted we all wait in the car, before escorting Laura to the backroom to oversee the bartering process. After the deal was done, a few of us decided we actually wanted a little more spending money and stopped at a normal currency-exchange kiosk in the center of Ulaanbaatar. We received about half as many tugriks to the dollar for our trouble. With cash in our pockets we were like little kids at a carnival. We bought some "ancient Mongolian artifacts" that Batzorig told us were definitely fakes, some weird little statues of fat wrestlers, jewelry, various camel-hair trivets, kids' toys, and a couple sets of "goat ankle bone fortune tellers" called "shagai", which consisted of a model ger (you know the Mongolian yurt you stayed in at that eco-resort? It's another bastardization of their language – they are actually called "gers") made of wood, a 3" x 5" camel-hair "rolling" mat, four goat ankle bones, and a hilariously translated guide to reading your fortune based on how the bones fall after you roll them.

The instructions for this ancient art were printed on a glossy directions sheet, and I have to believe that something was lost in translation. They started with the story of a man who lost a horse, who then, for reasons unexplained, threw some animal ankle bones a number of times until the bones told him (again, unexplained how they told him) that the horse was "inside him" and safe and would come back in two days. And guess what, everyone? It was safe! And it did come back in two days! No word on whether it had been inside him. This man then told everyone he knew that they should throw ankle bones to learn extremely accurate and specific future predictions about their life. The instructions went on to say that all one had to do to learn their future was to whisper a question to the bones, then throw them. The way they fell could then be compared to an equally confusingly translated chart to learn the answer.

The bones are roughly four-sided and each side has a name — Horse, Camel, Sheep, and Goat. Four sides and four bones mean, mathematically, that there are only 35 possible non-repeating permutations. Each of those combinations (horse, camel, sheep, goat for instance) had a corresponding prediction — actually, only 32 of them did, and there was a note reading: "If you roll something other than these combinations, roll the bones again".

After whispering a few questions to the bones, such as "Will *Beast Hunter* be a massive hit?" and "Will we find a beautiful Mongolian woman who has a thing for British film crews?", we received our incredibly confusing answers:

"Gossips and quarrels"
"More gossips and bad quarrels"
"Things are on your side, but not completely"
and
"Outside force will influence you"

We were happy to find that "One will come and arrive soon" when we asked the pretty-lady question, but alas, just as we had no gossip or bad quarrels, we also had no women under the age of 85 visit our camp.

We refrained from buying anything that had the potential to get us detained at the airport, or that we had some moral qualms with, like the preserved head of a golden eagle or various other endangered species parts, snake wine (a dead snake in a bottle of vodka), and "inactive" Soviet-era bombs, grenades, and AKs. I did purchase an "ancient Buddhist knife", at which Batzorig just shook his head and smiled, saying, "I hope this wasn't much US money." It was not much US money, but did almost get me detained in Moscow on the way home. I also bought my wife, Anna, an "ancient Mongolian necklace", which received a similar response from Batzorig and has never been worn by her.

While part of the trip to the market was for tat, we did have a mission, and was one the Brits on the crew found hysterical. They dubbed it "Operation Pat's Pants" – "pants" being British-English for underwear. We needed to get me a special outfit and some underwear to go with it. Our production team had a plan to quickly indoctrinate me into Mongolian nomadic culture/society and it involved large, sweaty, nearly naked men and some tighty-whities. I was going to wrestle in the Naadam festival, also known as "The Three Games of Men", and I needed to look just right for my big day.

Naadam is the biggest event of the year for the nomads of Mongolia. It's a festival, carnival, marketplace and excuse to get together with "neighbors" who might live a couple hundred miles away. We referred to it, as respectfully as possible, as "festivus" because of the feats of strength associated with it. Unlike most holidays in the US, the main event at Naadam is the competitions – the Three Games of Men in fact: archery, horseback riding, and wrestling. Women have started participating in the first two, but there are no female wrestlers. Each event is a throwback to the Mongolia of antiquity where the participants don traditional clothing and use ceremonial equipment, sometimes handed down for countless generations. Before we left for Mongolia, the series director had sent me an email that said simply, "Get ready," with a picture of a very buff Mongolian man wearing super-fancy boots, a tiny Speedo, a beanie hat that appeared to have a golden penis rising from it, and a bedazzled "shirt" that only covered his shoulders, with a rope tied around his bulging six-pack abs.

I thought he was joking. He was not. Batzorig was very excited for me to wrestle. He said it was a great honor for the town to have me, "a famous American", participate. I tried to dissuade him of this misconception but he kept insisting how much Mongolians love Nat Geo. It was humbling, and I told him it was I who was honored to be invited to participate, and hoped I wouldn't do the tradition an injustice. He assured me that as long as I looked the part, people would love me. He said that we could get everything we needed at the market. When I asked about the efficacy of the Speedo, he said with no embarrassment, "Some men wear nothing under them, but this is risky. Pieces may fall out and everyone laughs. It is very funny and part of the joy of the games." If I wanted to prevent "pieces" falling out, he recommended tighty-whities, which I did not own, being a boxer-brief guy. Thus, "Operation Pat's Pants" was born.

We wandered through the market, picking up our trinkets and a few old Russian military uniforms to use in reenactments later in the episode, and finally found my "pants" at a stand selling undergarments. Laura made a big scene of asking the kind old woman at the stand what size she thought I'd need, stating that I only knew American sizes. She held various-sized briefs up to my crotch before selecting the one she assured us would offer me the most support and comfort. Then it was time for the wrestling outfit. We located a few stands selling what we would need. I was told that the "shirt" was called a "zodog" and looked the way it did for a very particular reason. According to legend, at some point in history a wrestler beat everyone in the competition, then ripped open their zodog to reveal her breasts, showing everyone that she was a woman. From then on, the zodog has had to be open-fronted so that you can see the wrestler's chest. No one seemed to know why they needed this complex article of clothing rather than just going shirtless, which also exposes your breasts, if you have them, or just letting women compete since, you know, it's the twenty-first century.

The briefs are called "shuudag" and are designed for increased mobility and to prevent another wrestler from grabbing any loose clothing. I assume this is why Hulk Hogan also wore Speedos all through the 1980s, and not just to mentally scar a generation of children. There was no risk of anyone grabbing any loose bits in these briefs. They were *tight*. The boots were called "gutal" and were designed specifically for wrestling, with leather strings on the sides rather than upfront. The boots were beautiful, but unfortunately out of our budget, so Batzorig said I could borrow a pair from another wrestler on the day of the event.

The hat that appeared to all our eyes to be adorned with a golden phallus was intended to strike fear in your opponent, a strategy also employed by proboscis monkeys who wave their genitals at other males as a threat. The protrusion ended in a knot, which was supposed to symbolize you tying your opponent like a pretzel. I saw no chance of this happening, but,

I would look the part.

The stand we finally settled on was run by an older woman and her attractive daughter, who looked to be about 25. As a general rule, Mongolian people are beautiful. Many of the people we met would be extremely successful models in America with their tall, muscular frames and unusually angular yet round faces. Batzorig seemed to know these two and struck up a conversation. The woman looked me up and down and tossed me a shirt and briefs, then continued speaking in Mongolian to Batzorig. The conversation paused and he looked at me and said, "Well?"

"Well what?"

"Are you going to try them on?"

"Oh, yeah, I guess I should. Where do I do that?"

"What do you mean?"

"Is there a changing room or something?"

"What is this changing room?"

"Where do I try them on?"

"What do you mean? Try them on, please. We need to make sure they fit. C'mon."

"Um, right here? Is that okay?"

We were standing in a very crowded outdoor market with hundreds of people all around us. I guessed this was no time to be modest. I stripped off my shirt and tried on the zodog. It certainly revealed my chest. There was no way I could hide boobs while wearing this. It was sort of a belly-shirt, like Tommy on the cover of the first Ramones album, but with the entire front removed. It covered my shoulders and arms, and half my back. The young woman giggled and helped me tie it. They tossed me a few hats before finding the right size and commenting on my smaller-than-anticipated head.

So there I stood, in my zodog, golden phallus hat, and oversized camouflage cargo pants. My crew and the two women looked at me expectantly. It was clear it was time to ditch the pants. I dropped my pants and was grateful that I was wearing black boxer-briefs underneath. It still felt strange. They tossed me pair after pair of shuudags and kept reminding me that, "they are supposed to fit very snug. You don't want any pieces to pop out." The woman and her daughter helped tie the sides of each pair (they have rope on the sides that tighten them), and remarked that I looked "very fierce". As James, Laura, and our cameraman Brendan went into fits of laughter with each pose I struck, I felt far from fierce. I was, after all, wearing tiny blue or red bikini briefs over a pair of black boxer-briefs. I had settled on a blue zodog and asked if the shuudag needed to match (both traditionally come in either blue or red). Batzorig thought this was very funny, but never answered my question. I ended up with both in blue, but a red, black, and gold hat. The best wrestlers' hats had yellow lines on them indicating their rank – the more lines, the higher the rank. My hat would be bare.

I had my uniform, we had our tat, and we were ready for Naadam. On the way back into the city where we would hopefully be reunited with our luggage and catch a plane to a rural outpost in the inner Gobi Desert, Batzorig gave me wrestling advice. He told me about the history of the games and their significance in their culture. He encouraged me to listen to the songs that the wrestlers and the crowd sang in response (I was reassured that I would not be expected to sing) which were very poetic and compared the wrestlers to beautiful eagles, sunrises and sunsets, told the stories of Chinggis' horses, and told a story about a man who shot his younger brother because he thought he was a gazelle while he was wearing his traditional wrestling outfit. I didn't really understand that last part, but it sounded moving none the less.

He told me about strategy and past high-profile wrestlers. I found that the top wrestler in the country is carried on the crowd's shoulders and presented to the president of Mongolia, who bestows on him the greatest title in all sports

– "The Undefeatable Giant of the Nation". I wanted to be the Undefeatable Giant of a Nation, but there was little chance of my winning even one match, and even if I somehow managed to win at our games, because I was competing in a "country" match – meaning far outside the capital – the highest title I could be granted was "Soum's Elephant", which was still pretty awesome. I learned that wrestlers have a coach of sorts called a zasuul, and whose main role is to hold the wrestler's hat (which contains the wrestler's soul while they wrestle) and slap their butt if they seem tired. Again, I didn't really understand any of this, and was now certain I would make a fool of myself – the best possible outcome seemed to be me losing without insulting the crowd.

Our team assured me that wrestling was a good strategy. They said that just by participating I was sure to earn some favor in the eyes of the locals. Since it was exceptionally unlikely that we would find a death worm, our best bet for the purposes of filming was to find people who had seen it and interview them, then, if they told us a detailed enough story, we could put a reenactment over their words and show the viewing public what they had experienced. The purpose of this series was less to "find" the beast in each episode and more to "hunt" it – to tell its story, bring it into the light, show why its story is important to the people we were with, and the place we were in. As a Nat Geo series, sense of place was always critical. No one on the crew had grown up in these locations, though – no one knew enough to provide the cultural and historical context for the remarkable stories we were hearing. We relied on the folks we interviewed and our amazing fixers for that. My main job as the host was to always make the person I was interviewing feel comfortable and open – to show them respect and gain their trust. I needed them to treat me like an old friend and spare no detail. The cultural divide here was huge, as was the language barrier. Each episode challenged the producers and me to come up with a way to bridge this chasm. It usually involved me eating some gastrointestinal-distress-inducing foods or making a fool out of myself – and Mongolia would be no different. If I participated in traditional Mongolian wrestling, win or lose (I want to stress here that no one, at any point in the planning or execution of this, thought I would win – no one. Not the crew, my wife, Batzorig, or myself), I would show everyone we met that I was respectful of their customs and happy to put myself through just about anything to be a part of their world, even for a moment.

The plan here was for me to watch a few matches, get changed into my outfit, get some coaching from a local champion wrestler, then head into the ring and put what I'd learned into practice. We still had another day in the capital before any of this, though, so I put it out of my mind as, early the next morning, we went to the airport to retrieve our luggage and filming gear. We were informed that it had arrived as expected on that day's flight from Moscow.

The main thing we needed to film on that last day in Ulaanbaatar was the famous Gandantegchinlen Monastery, a beautiful Buddhist temple where a large number of monks-in-training live. We walked around, lit some incense, and spun some prayer wheels, I caught a few lizards, and Brendan filmed some great B-roll, which consists of scene-establishing images. Shots of kids playing, beautiful vistas, animals running, crowds of people walking and talking – the shots you see when the scenes change from one location to another, or when the voiceover is describing something necessary to the story, but also kind of boring – these shots take a massive amount of time to collect and require a very talented, dedicated camera person willing to wake up before dawn to get a sunrise shot, or babysit a camera for hours while it captures a spider spinning a web. Brendan was this kind of camera person, and our B-roll was shockingly beautiful in this episode.

James and I bought eight bags of breadcrumbs from a little kid to throw to the pigeons to get them to fly over and over and over so Brendan could capture a few seconds of footage. One of the things I loved about being in a Buddhist country was the respect and love for all living things. I'm always shocked by the comments you hear people make about pigeons – they consider them lower than cockroaches. In some cities, if you are caught feeding a pigeon you can be issued a fine, and in most people will make nasty comments. Here, though, pigeons were celebrated as the rock doves they truly are and everyone around us was happy to see us feeding them.

A quick aside about pigeons, because they really are fascinating birds. They are rock doves, native to the rocky islands and cliffs of North Africa and Europe's coast. Evolving on such rocky outcrops gave them incredible anatomical adaptations, namely being able to slam their faces into rocks all day and not develop brain damage, destroy their beaks, or die. This trait made them perfectly suited to urban life as they are one of the few birds that can feed on blacktop and cement. They're also one of the smartest birds – they can recognize each letter of the English alphabet and individual humans, and are one of the few animal species who can pass the "mirror test", which demonstrates self-realization.

After feeding the birds we were ready for the monks. We entered one building in the temple complex and saw about 75 monks hanging out – it was a sea of saffron robes and shaved heads. It was funny to see monks on their cell phones. Many had iPhones and appeared to be surfing the web, while others were texting, talking, or playing games like Candy Crush. It was even funnier to see no less than four turn to check out a young woman while they were supposed to be chanting. We chatted with them for a little while before filming, just asking them about life in Mongolia. They seemed like a good group of guys. Most were fairly well traveled, having visited multiple

European countries, while some had been to America and nearly all had been to China, Russia, and all over Mongolia. I asked them about animals and was directed to a couple monks in their mid-thirties who were the real wildlife lovers of the group. These guys had stories about wolves, snow leopards, eagles, snakes, and lizards, They knew all of the local wildlife and lots of cool legends. One hesitantly told me how much he loved Nat Geo. A few others overheard and chimed in. They hummed the *Explorer* theme and started laughing. It just goes to show what a truly respected organization Nat Geo really is, and made me feel even more privileged to have my name associated with theirs. We gave the monks a bunch of Nat Geo hats and thanked them for talking to us, then filmed some beautiful footage of them chanting.

I tried on my wrestling outfit before dinner that night. I didn't have boots, but I figured my flip-flops were close enough. I ran downstairs to our hotel lobby and greeted the crew, saying, "Okay, where are we going to eat?" Everyone, even Batzorig, busted out laughing. I looked ridiculous, and borderline obscene. After dancing to some EDM that James had pulled up on his phone, I went upstairs to get changed.

Early the next morning we were on a tiny prop plane heading out to the middle of the Gobi Desert. The only other people on the plane were workers at a local copper mine. The short flight was surprisingly awesome. Despite being in the air less than three hours, they fed us twice. Bizarre little sandwiches with unknown contents – some seemed like meat and jam, others were fish and something like mustard, but not quite the same. We also received huge bags of candy-coated peanuts and lots of orange juice. It was better service, and better food, than I have ever received from most major American aviation companies, whose names I will not mention.

When we touched down in the middle of the Gobi we were in a rush. We had lost a day waiting for the luggage in Ulaanbaatar and were now arriving on the day of Naadam rather than the day before it. We deboarded the plane and walked across cracking tarmac to the tiniest airport I have ever been in. The entire building was about the size of my living room. There were three military officers, two men with buzz cuts and a woman with severe bangs sternly overseeing the operation. There was also one civilian airline worker. The room was very hot, even with a car-sized, condensation-dripping air conditioner hooked up to a window. We watched as our stewardesses and pilot unloaded our luggage and started carrying it into the building, a couple pieces at a time. The other passengers (there were about 10) lined up and put their hands behind their backs like a military drill. We didn't know what was happening, so we did the same. The one civilian airline worker, a pudgy Mongolian man with lots of product slicking down his black hair and making it stick to his head, smiled as he administered a breathalyzer to each passenger in turn. We all looked at each other, very confused.

One of the military personnel motioned for us to step out of line. The taller of the two men explained that these passengers were going to work in the copper mine and had to prove that they weren't drunk. James asked whether it mattered if we were drunk (it was about 8:30am). The guard did not smile, but confirmed that no one cared if we were drunk. Laura corrected him, saying that she cared very much if any of us were drunk before 9am. We grabbed our bags, handed the military woman our declaration cards, and exited the airport.

Waiting for us outside were two amazing vehicles: an electric blue minivan and a grey, rusting UAZ-452, the Soviet-era equivalent of a VW bus. It was kitted out with off-road tires and massive shocks, and smelled strongly of gasoline. We threw our gear in the minivan and hopped in what James dubbed the "Soviet Mystery Machine". There were many loose wires hanging from the console and one under the steering wheel would occasionally emit some sparks. When we asked the driver if the sparking wire was dangerous – because, you know, we could smell a gas leak – he simply said, "Yes, do not touch anything," and kept going.

The Gobi is massive and very sparsely populated. I think people understand that intellectually, but in reality – holy shit, the Gobi is *massive* and *very* sparsely populated. We drove for over an hour without seeing any sign of life. Nothing – not a bird, no old soda can, no roads. Honestly, one of the most bizarre things about my time in the Gobi was the lack of roads, but that all drivers somehow knew exactly where to go without a compass or navigating by the stars. It was like they had an innate sense of direction driving them to reach the next human habitation. I have a terrible sense of direction. My best friend Adam used to think it was funny to ask me to "point towards the ocean" – he would do this when the ocean was about two blocks away and we were indoors. I would inevitably guess and he would say something like, "Okay, but you have to go through Canada first," or "Eventually, but you're pointing west and the Atlantic is literally 100 yards in the other direction." Dom, another of my closest friends whom I frequently camp with, is constantly amazed by my inability to read a map, use a compass, or sense what direction we should turn. He thought I was joking until one hike when he refused to lead and subsequently followed me for hours as we wandered aimlessly (despite being less than a quarter-mile from the parking lot). I was consistently amazed at the ability of our drivers to find where we were going. They would turn at a right angle, for no apparent reason, then turn again, etc., and always found our destination.

And it wasn't like they were making turns at rock formations. This was the Gobi Desert, it looked exactly the same in every direction, stretching out to the horizon at times. Anyway, this first trip was breathtaking. I had never seen a place so formidable. There were rocky crags, towering, porous-looking mountains, miles and miles of scrub brush, sand dunes, and the hottest sun I have ever experienced. We would come over a ridge and suddenly the entire landscape would change to patches of trees with smaller plants and rabbits around them, with vultures circling overhead. Then over another hill and there would be nothing, just sand. It was such a strange and beautiful landscape, unlike anywhere else on Earth.

After another hour we cleared a huge rocky hill and a tiny town appeared in the distance. People use the expression "the middle of nowhere" pretty liberally. This town was in the middle of nowhere. It was a village surrounded by uninhabited scrub as far as the eye could see in every direction. It seemed to be about a half-mile around and consisted of maybe two dozen buildings and houses – only one building was more than a story tall. The entire town looked dusty and faded, like an Old West settlement crossed with Soviet-style concrete-block houses. There were no trees, but I saw some brush and scrub plants. There were no paved roads, and no roads of any sort leading to the village from any direction.

We parked and immediately scrambled to get our kit unpacked and assembled, and check in at the only hotel in town – which was also the only bank, general store, and restaurant. It was the three-story building, and we found out it had no toilets, and although it did have a few sinks, it lacked running water. Without even going to our rooms we walked to the town center, just outside of the fence surrounding our hotel, which was filling fast with nomads and horses.

Our rush to be on time for this festival was not just the normal rush of a film crew trying to capture every possible moment. We had actually asked the local government to hold off a couple days on celebrating Naadam in the region we were in so that we could be there to film it. And they said yes! Imagine someone asking Boston to move the 4th of July a couple days because they wanted to be there for it, and having them agree. This was the biggest festival of the year – and they had moved it for us. After asking for a favor like that, it would have been pretty horrible of us to show up late or not at all. Luckily, it looked like we had made it just in time.

The nomads had traveled extreme distances to get to this little outpost and celebrate Naadam. Naadam is a big deal in the cities in Mongolia, but it's the event of the year in these small outpost towns in the Gobi. It's the one time of the year that all of the nomads who are normally scattered hundreds of miles apart get together. They arrived from all directions by horse, off-road cars similar to ours, motorbikes, trucks, minivans, and all manner of vehicles. Some were towing horse carriages, others were laden with goods to be sold at the festival; some were dressed in jeans, button-down shirts, and cowboy hats, others in traditional Mongolian garb. It was a hodgepodge of cultures, ages, and traditions. The faces in the crowd were fascinating. The older Mongolians looked regal, their angular, round faces deeply lined and tanned. The kids were adorable and I was told by Batzorig, and many others that, "Mongolian children are the most independent and fastest learners on Earth." We had parents proudly tell us about their potty-trained three-month-old children – they would hold it until the parents brought them outside and removed their pants – only then would the babies obediently pee and poop in the sand. The parents would then clean them up and take them back inside. No diapers needed. We witnessed this for ourselves several times. As a new parent at the time of this writing, I am more in awe of this feat than almost anything else I witnessed while filming the series. At the festival we saw kids embracing, having possibly not seen each other for a year. There were teenagers awkwardly greeting each other, adult friends hugging and laughing – it was beautiful, and was easy to get wrapped up in the excitement. People noticed us, but didn't pay much attention other than a polite nod or a handshake.

From the time the first nomad showed up it couldn't have

been more than two hours until the town center (which was a gravel-covered patch of flat land about as large as two football fields) was packed with hundreds of people who circled it and made a sort of odd-shaped "ring". People were talking, drinking, eating, cooking, laughing, visiting, etc. Event organizers were setting up giant speakers and handing out microphones. Those who would be participating in the games were getting ready. Small children were dressing ponies in traditional Mongolian horse decorations and getting dressed themselves, while adults were doing the same for horseback riding and archery, which seemed to be the first events.

The festival started with a very loud crack of microphone feedback followed by a rousing, national anthem-like song. No one stood up during it, or acknowledged it any way, really. I awkwardly put my hand over my heart, because I thought I saw another man doing this. Turns out he was just scratching his chest. I kept my hand on my heart and tried to appear confident in my decision. After that, an announcer who was clearly in the school of 1980s WWF announcing came on and did his best, "Let's get ready to RUUUUMMMMBBBBBLLLLEEEE," in Mongolian.

First up was kids' archery and horseback riding, at the same time. While the horses rode around the edges of the ring, small, adorable children in traditional clothing lined up and fired arrows at targets. I thought it would be best to keep my eyes on the archers, as many arrows were going astray and landing dangerously close to some spectators. This seemed like the direction danger was likely to come from, until I was almost run down by a six-year-old on a horse. You needed to keep your head on a swivel in the children's portion of the games. It was unclear how the horsemanship portion was being judged – or if it was being judged – but it ended as abruptly as it started with the announcer declaring a "winner" – a girl who looked to be about seven. A bunch of little kids then ran out onto the field in wrestling outfits and started to throw each other to the ground to the general amusement of all watching. There didn't seem to be any points system, but they were clearly having a good time, as was the cheering crowd. The archery continued nearby until suddenly it didn't and a winner was announced.

It was all very confusing and happening really fast. Adults then made loops on horseback – some riding very close to the adult archers who were now on the field. The wrestling was still kids, and I noticed that a few of the older boys were wearing sweatpants. I couldn't imagine being in that awkward 12-year-old phase and expected to wear bikini briefs in front of this crowd. I was the kid who wore a T-shirt when swimming until high school – I absolutely would have been the kid wrestling in sweatpants. I started cheering for one of them until I discovered my favorite wrestler. There was a kid who looked to be about 10 or 11 with spiked hair, Oakley knock-offs, a Notorious B.I.G. T-shirt, bright-red Adidas trackpants, and traditional boots wrestling a much more muscular boy of about the same age, in traditional attire. A man near me saw me staring and said, "He forgot his clothes at home." No way did this kid forget his clothes! He knew exactly what he was doing. This was psychological warfare, and it was – oh no, Biggie Smalls was slammed, hard, to the gravel. When he got up he was crying a little. The guy that beat him slapped the kid's butt good-naturedly, then they both ran off the field.

When not dodging arrows or narrowly avoiding being trampled by horses, I walked around the crowd. I found that everyone was enjoying Mongolia's version of carnival food – sheep knuckles and fermented mare's milk. The sheep knuckles were basically a handful of meat, tendon, and bone which one holds in their palm and gnaws on, slurping, sucking, spitting, and trying to tear away as much flesh as possible. People really seemed to be enjoying them. I bought one and have to say the meat was really good, and just like blue crab in Maryland, getting to it is part of the fun. You have to just let the inherent messiness of the process wash over you and make your peace with it. You're going to end up with sheep cartilage in your hair – deal with it.

The chaos of Naadam continued. As the adult riders continued to circle the field and the unnecessarily loud announcer continued... talking? Calling plays? Commenting on the games? I honestly have no idea what he was doing, but he was doing it loudly, while the kids who had been wrestling started posing for pictures and a winner was announced. It was a four-year-old boy who was crying hysterically until his father (who looked like a very good-natured, paunchy, businessman type) ran out on the field and picked him up on his shoulders. Everyone cheered and the kid started laughing and lifting his arms up *Rocky* style. Then all the kids from the three events ran back out on the field as the adult archers finished. I think someone won – maybe not, I really couldn't tell. The riders also dismounted and some of them started singing – again, I don't know if there was a winner. None were really doing tricks or racing, they were just riding horses in different directions around the field, through the field, out into the desert and back, and then dismounting and singing. I was very confused. All of this had lasted about an hour and a half.

It then became apparent that wrestling was the main event, and the previous 90 minutes of chaos had been the warm-up act. A few dozen extremely muscular Mongolian men who ranged in age from about 15-40 walked out on the field to roars and cheers from the crowd and announcer, who led the crowd in a couple songs while, to my amazement, the men danced a sort of semi-choreographed number in their traditional clothing. They stamped their feet, held their arms out like birds' wings, and twirled, in unison, occasionally flapping. It was surreal. Then they went back to stretching and talking with each other as the songs continued.

The next bit happened very quickly. I was watching the show from the sidelines when a giant Mongolian man in an electric blue kimono and no pants grabbed me and picked me up like I was a child. I let out a little whimper of fear and confusion as he carried me into a tent on the sidelines of the field. My crew followed, so I hoped that this was the plan and I wasn't being abducted. He put me down and began flexing at me, like, intimidation style. I smiled, although I was very frightened. Our producer seemed nonplussed and instructed Brendan to keep filming. The man continued to flex and grimace. I stood awkwardly smiling at him. He had to be 6'3" and a good 300 pounds. He was pure muscle and looked like he could rip my arms off and beat me to death with them. He had a broad, angular face with very defined cheekbones, a square jaw, and small eyes. His nose looked like it had been broken a couple times. I would not have messed with this dude at a bar. This large man took his kimono off and revealed a wrestling outfit. Excellent, I thought, this must be my coach. Okay, time to learn a few moves and get changed. I was a little nervous, but feeling good.

The giant and a few other men then started taking off all of my clothes. He lifted me into the air from behind as a guy pulled my boots off, then spun me around and another man ripped off my shirt while two others started undoing my belt and pulling my pants down and laughing. I kept trying to make eye contact with anyone from our crew. I was really hoping this was part of the plan and I wasn't being sexually assaulted. Finally I saw James, who was barely keeping it together. He was nearly doubled over laughing. I noticed Laura, who was just staring open-mouthed, and heard our producer saying, "Okay, this is different. Yes, keep filming. I wonder what they'll do next. This is more aggressive than I'd thought, but it looks great." Once I was down to my underwear – the tighty-whities we had purchased the day before – the men stepped away and just looked at me. For some reason this was more awkward and terrifying than when they were ripping my clothes off. I just felt so exposed. I also looked like a child next to the giant.

After quietly assessing my nearly naked body for far too long, my blue shuudag booty shorts appeared, and when I tried to put them on I was pushed back by the laughing men. I tried again, and again I was pushed off balance. Okay, it seemed like it was some sort of hazing, maybe? The giant stepped forward, took the briefs, and held them for me to step into. As I did, he picked me up in the air by the drawstrings on either side of the pants and shook me. Everyone roared with laughter. I was laughing too, but it was a bit higher pitched than it would have been seconds before. He then tied the sides, shaking each to make sure it was secure. I was then likewise "helped" into my shirt, the rope was tied around my lack of abs, and I was in the air again. Ornate (but far too small), pointy-toed green leather boots were placed on my feet and tied up. The finishing touch was the golden penis hat, which Laura placed on my head.

Laura then said, "There has actually been a slight change of plans. You aren't going to practice; you're just going to wrestle."

"What? Now?"

"Pat, look at these guys, do you really think practicing would make a difference?"

She was right. There was no way I was being crowned Soum's Elephant.

"Okay, that's fine. So the giant – is he my coach? My Zeus? You know, the guy who holds my soul and slaps my ass?"

"Um, no. Actually, he's your opponent. He's the favorite to win."

"Yeah, no shit. Of course he's gonna beat me, look at him."

"No, I mean, he's the favorite to win the entire games."

"Oh, perfect."

"*That* is your zasuul," said Laura, and she pointed to a very kindly and confused-looking older man who inclined his head to me in greeting. I walked over and asked if he spoke English, and was pleased to find that he did. He had a calm, soothing voice and seemed to be enjoying himself, even if he was confused as to how he got mixed up with the likes of me. He was a former wrestler, he told me, but now really enjoyed his new role as coach.

I heard the announcer say something that elicited very loud cheering and applause and my opponent ran onto the field with a sort of effortless jog. No physical activity I have ever performed could be described as "effortless" by an onlooker. My coach pushed me towards the opening of the tent and onto the field. I started to jog and felt my, well, everything, bounce. "Oh God, something is going to pop out."

My coach walked next to me and said, sternly, "Dance."

"Excuse me?"

The crowd was singing.

"Dance. Dance now. Dance like an eagle."

"I thought eagles flew? How do they dance?"

"Dance, now, like an eagle."

So I did. I began my eagle dance, and the crowd laughed, a lot. I was later told this was because I didn't flap my arms; rather, I "danced like a plane". I still hold to the fact that when I think "eagle" I think "majestic soaring." There was nothing majestic about my dance, but I did soar – I soared the shit out of that dance. My hat was then removed by my coach, who once again reminded me that it contained my soul. What did that mean? To this day I don't know. Maybe my soul is still in that hat. (I think it's now on the CEO of Icon Films Harry Marshall's wall. Does that mean Harry owns my soul?)

All thoughts of being devoid of a soul left my head as I stared at the nearly naked, nationally ranked, giant Mongolian standing in front of me. I began circling him, and by that I mean I put my hands in an "I'm gonna get you" position like you play with little kids, took two steps to the left, and was immediately grabbed by him. He held my shoulders like I was a child and knocked my legs out from under me with one motion. ("Sweep the leg, Johnny!") I was then thrown, hard, onto my side on the rocky ground. Everyone clapped politely. My opponent helped me up, untied my shirt, made a big display of slapping my butt – like, leaned me over, wound up, and slapped – waved to the crowd (who cheered), and pointed toward the tent, evidently sending me back there. I jogged to my coach who put my hat back on me and continued to the tent to catcalls, applause, and lots of laughter.

I was so confused. A few of the thoughts running through my head were: What just happened? Did he really just spank me? Did I lose in less than a minute? Why did he untie my shirt? People began coming over and taking pictures with me, and all of them put one hand firmly on my butt when the pictures were taken. I still don't know if that was normal, but at least 15 people took pictures with me and all of them grabbed my ass. The picture was from the front – what I mean by that is, they were not pictures *of* people grabbing my ass, they just happened to be doing it as the picture was taken.

Laura appeared and frantically said, "You're up again, now," and I was shoved back into the ring. What was happening? I was only supposed to wrestle once. I had lost – that had to be enough embarrassment for one day. Maybe Brendan had missed it? It did happen really fast. I found out later that my opponent had been asked to go light on me. After the match he said, "I did, he just fell so easy." Now, though, the announcer was saying something that made the crowd go into hysterics. After it was all over, I was told it was: "The American doesn't believe that he did his best, so we are going to give him another shot. This time, he will wrestle a child." And wrestle a child I did. A skinny 16-year-old boy came out, danced like an eagle and wrestled me.

As soon as I saw him I thought of Chris Hansen from *To*

Catch a Predator.

"Oh, it's you again, Pat. What're you doing way out here in Mongolia where Americans probably assume that the statutory laws are somewhat hazy? Last time we met you were pooping in front of a bunch of kids in Cameroon. Now I find you here, practically naked, wearing a very interesting hat, about to lock arms with and wrestle a sweaty young child. I'm sure it's not what it looks like, right?"

I figured I would make the best of a bad situation. This was like fighting a girl in grade school – if you won, everyone would make fun of you, and rightfully look down on you for hitting a girl, but if you lost – holy shit, a girl beat you up? I wanted to win. The damage was already done, after all – I was fighting a child. I did last a little longer than I had against the giant, I even took a couple swipes at his legs, which the crowd loved. But in the end he threw me to the ground, untied my shirt, and made a real showing of raising his hand up high, dramatically, and slapping my ass. I was beaten by a child, hard.

For the rest of the trip multiple drunken men approached me and mimed my now famous wrestling scene. On two separate occasions they tried to drag me out of retirement and get me to wrestle. I was terrified, thinking these large, drunk guys actually wanted to fight me, until they started re-enacting my eagle dance and laughing – apparently it was a huge hit. I didn't wrestle either of them, but they did seem to appreciate the fact that I had tried it, and everyone who saw or heard about my moves treated me like one of their own.

After being beaten by the child and leaving the ring, a fellow wrestler offered me the goat knuckle he was currently chewing on. I thanked him, grabbed it, bit a few chunks off and swilled some mare's milk. He patted me on the back and invited me to sit with the other guys who had lost. They shared anecdotes, traditions, food, and drinks with me. Being humiliated and having my butt slapped a couple times was a small price to pay for the trust it had garnered. I found out that most of the crowd thought I had let the boy win, which they all told me was very kind of me.

I saw the kid who beat me again about a week later. He had become somewhat of a celebrity because of our encounter, and thanked me profusely for letting him win. I told him I had absolutely not let him win, and in fact tried my hardest to beat him. He laughed, thinking I was joking, and thanked me again, shaking my hand over and over. We joked around a little and took a couple pictures. He definitely seemed different – more confident, and somehow older. When he left, Batzorig spoke to his family and told me, "He will marry well after beating you. He is very respected, and lots of women like him now." That made me really happy. Good for that kid. God knows, I could have used a boost in that department when I was 16.

Chapter 2

"Oh God! Don't Eat the Fudge!"

There's a chapter in the Mokele M'bembe book from this series about toilets and bodily functions and body parts that go down a lowbrow rabbit hole which I'm not entirely proud of, but that has nothing on this chapter. I mean, this isn't a *50 Shades* knockoff, but it certainly isn't *Portrait of an Artist* either. Anyone who has spent a fair amount of time with factions of men knows that, as a group, we can be a pretty disgusting bunch. Under most conditions, societal norms, the desire to impress potential mates, fear of being ostracized or imprisoned, and some good old Catholic guilt tend to keep our foul, foul natures in check. However, when you travel to incredibly remote regions of the world, keeping company almost exclusively with other foul-mouthed men, spend the majority of your days in surreal, often very hot and sweaty situations, and only sleep four hours a night at best, these inhibitions have a way of disappearing in a manner that would alarm any sane observer. They would think that all of us are perpetually on the verge of sacrificing one of our own to the *Lord of the Flies*.

Simply stated, we tend to egg each other on and encourage more and more crass behavior. If you think *Superbad* and *The Inbetweeners* were over the top and the conversations are unbelievable and exaggerated, you have never spent time with a film crew. I also have to say that what I'm describing is not Toxic Masculinity or the now infamous "locker room talk," both of which are abhorrent to everyone I've ever worked with or considered a friend. I am describing toilet humor and gross-out crassness, simple and pure in its filth. Our collective obscenity really hit its stride in Mongolia, and left a permanent greasy streak on my brain.

Our crew on that shoot was, however, not all male – but that fact did nothing to stem the tide of crassness. Lady Laura of Clifton Wood was our associate producer. She earned the title of "Lady" Laura by being just about as unlady-like as possible. (Even though I'd argue against the term "ladylike", but you know what I mean.) She is, as seems to be a prerequisite for working at Icon, remarkable in every way. She adapted to any situation with ease – going from arguing with a porter who was ripping us off, to exhibiting the poise and grace of a royal, as her name implies, back to discussing the proper technique for using a squat toilet after some really sketchy undercooked meat. She was definitely the most genial on the crew, but could also be as raunchy as anyone and would often start a conversation in a cockney accent: "Oi, chappy. Wha'we inta ta-dai, China?" She taught me about rhyming slang. Somehow, China = plate, which rhymes with "mate", and mate means "buddy". I never got it. She immediately felt like a long-lost relative.

Being a woman got her no special treatment from us (and she wouldn't have taken it if we'd tried), but being a very attractive young woman did get her a lot of special treatment from our guides, which we all benefited from. She's average height, right around my age, pale and freckly with a devilish grin and piercing grey-blue eyes. She normally wears her long, curly auburn hair pulled back in a ponytail. Just as a — ahem — completely unrelated aside, while receiving a formal education in English slang I learned that the "T word" isn't as offensive in England as it is in the States and is pronounced to rhyme with "flat" rather than "blot". I will not, however, ever feel comfortable saying it, no matter how many times it was shouted at me with various accents.

Most of the crew knew each other before the shoot – and we knew one another to be intelligent, progressive-minded, and very difficult to insult – meaning we felt comfortable enough to let the insults and foul language fly. James and Brendan, sound and cameraman respectively, had worked together on a bunch of *River Monsters* shoots and amassed a collection of embarrassing stories about each other. Combining the time we'd spent planning the shoots in Bristol, filming in Canada, NYC, Boston, and Massachusetts, James, Laura, and I had spent over a month together by the time we landed in Mongolia.

The first couple days in Mongolia were easy compared to our other shoots, and the jokes were just as safe. They consisted of long days exploring the capital city of Ulaanbaatar in a well-loved minibus guided by our diminutive fixer Batzorig, whose humor didn't stray beyond the work-safe territory of knock-knock jokes, usually with tourists as the butt of them. But as the Naadam festival approached, and we moved deeper into the Gobi Desert, we ditched the minibus and Batzorig's professional demeanor with it. He found it harder and harder to contain his excitement for the festival and began telling us how much fun we were in for. "There are many fun things to enjoy at Naadam! There are the 'Three Games of Men', of course, but there is also cooked goat, mare's milk, and vodka! The mare's milk is so delicious, and we love it. You may probably not love it, but you might."

Brendan, who was looking out the window of our Russian-military vehicle at the vast expanse of desert, asked, "What milk?"

"Mare's milk." Explained Batzorig, "It will have been made into alcohol. Not strong alcohol like vodka, which there will also be, but weak alcohol, like beer. Mare's milk is very delicious. It is salty, warm, sour, wonderful, and gives you diarrhea. We like it very much."

"Mamilk?" asked a still-confused Brendan. "What is Mamilk?"

"No," I said. "*Mare's* milk. Mare, like a horse."

"*Oh,*" said Brendan. "Horse's milk, got it."

Batzorig furrowed his brow. "No, no, not horse's milk. If you

34

drink horse's milk you are drinking semen. You can have this if you want, but it isn't nearly as delicious as mare's milk. Would you like to drink this? We can get you some horse's semen to drink. It makes you strong, they say."

We all stared, open-mouthed. "You... drink horse semen?" asked a bewildered James.

"Yes! Like I said, it is not as good as other drinks. I will get you some at Naadam."

I hadn't read about this in the books and articles I had browsed to brush up on the traditional Mongolian festival. None of them mentioned drinking horse ejaculate. "Batzorig, will we be asked to drink horse semen as part of the games? Is this expected?" I asked, fearing the answer, and realizing as I said it that it was a question I'd never expected to ask.

"Not *expected*, no, but since you mention it I think you would like to try it, yes? Experience Mongolia. You want to live like us you say. Maybe not. You have said 'yes', but looks like 'No'," he said, seeming a little dejected.

Silence. A long awkward silence. After a minute or so, James spoke up. "Batzorig, as part of the games, would it be the most authentic experience if Pat does this? Would he really be a part of the culture? If that's expected then it's expected, and I'm *sure* Pat will do what he needs to." I saw his grin spreading. "Well, TV's Pat Spain, what do you think? Will you try it, like a *real* presenter?"

I had no idea how to respond. I was running through various scenarios in my head. Would I offend people if I refused? If I didn't refuse, holy shit what would the online comments look like? Would it make me vomit? What would it taste like? I had never before thought about what horse semen might taste like or what effect drinking large quantities of it would have. These were not thoughts I wanted to have. I hadn't known it, but I had hoped to go my entire life without ever thinking much at all about horse semen beyond its role in creating new horses. Were there health risks associated with drinking it? Would it be from multiple horses, a blend, or a single varietal? I was betting that it would be very high in calories. I hated that I was thinking about the caloric content of horse semen. How much would I need to drink? Oh God, I bet it's a lot. Would it be served warm? Would it be better cold? It seemed like it might be better cold. Again, thoughts I had hoped to go my entire life without thinking.

Before I could respond, Batzorig busted out laughing. "Gahahahahah! Oh Pat! You are so funny! No! Of course we don't drink horse semen! No one does this! It is so funny! It is such a fun joke! I have heard other guides have convinced people to do this as a joke! It is so funny! I couldn't keep going, though. Oh, Hahhahahaha!"

Holy shit. Relief spread over me. I laughed, James laughed, we all laughed. I was left with the lingering thought that I had made up my mind that I would, in fact, drink horse semen if I needed to for this series. This seemed like something I couldn't mentally come back from. It was almost as bad as really doing it. I felt a little shame.

"Oh, you are funny. That was funny." Said a still chortling Batzorig, "No 'horse's milk' for you. But, mare's milk – there will be plenty of mare's milk, and you might love it. We Mongolians play a game with it. It is so fun!"

"Like a drinking game?" I ventured, happy to change the subject and hopefully purge the images of cups filled with horse sperm from my mind. I imagined they would serve it in Styrofoam cups for some reas – oh God, why was I still thinking about this?

"Yes!" said a very excited Batzorig. "Yes! A game where you drink! A drinking game of mare's milk."

"What's the game? I love drinking games," said an enthusiastic James.

"It is so fun! You gather in your ger and make a line in the middle which no one can cross. Then you drink as much mare's milk as you can. You drink and drink and drink, until you vomit and you go to the line as you vomit, but your vomit must fall *outside* of the ger. It is such a fun game."

"Fuck you, you're joking," said James with a look of "You're not fooling me with your bodily fluids stories again" (yes, that is a look you can give).

"No! It is a very fun game!" said an earnest Batzorig.

"Batzorig, that sounds terrible. That doesn't sound like a game at all," said Laura.

"Well, girls don't usually play," said Batzorig, rolling his eyes to the guys as if to say, "Women, right?", thinking we would of course be with him on the virtues of a vomit game.

"Well, of course not. That *seems* like a game only men would play," said a smug Laura.

"Yes. It's for the guys. It is so much fun," said Batzorig with a distant expression, as if fondly remembering many mare's milk-vomit filled nights in the desert with the boys. "But, we probably won't have time to play. Sometimes, it takes a long time for someone to vomit. You might go quick, but maybe not. Ah, it is too bad. Maybe later in your trip!"

Oh, there was something to look forward to. We rode the rest of the way in a slightly uncomfortable silence. I was still trying to purge certain images from my overactive brain. Batzorig, though, had broken the seal on inappropriate humor, and we were only too happy to indulge.

After a three-hour trip through the strikingly gorgeous Gobi, we saw a small outpost village appear in a valley as we crested a ridge. The town we were staying in was in the province of Ömnögovi and reminded me of images of feudal villages from the dark ages, minus the high walls often seen surrounding such places. There was absolutely nothing around it in any direction as far as you could see. It wasn't like a city in the US where an urban center gives way to exurban sprawl, then suburbs, then rural farmlands, and finally undisturbed wilderness. This outpost village went from urban straight to wilderness. And "urban" is being generous – there were about 50 one or two-story buildings and traditional gers surrounding a gravel-covered center about the size of a Chili's parking lot. This was also a playground for the kids in the village with a couple slides and a lone swing set. There were "streets", but there was something off about them – besides all fading into desert and being almost indistinguishable from the "off-road" area next to them, that is. I think it was that they weren't uniform in size or shape. They looked like all roads must have at some point in history, before people laid cobblestones. These "roads" were more "urban trails" and were created by foot and horse traffic, then a few had been retrofitted to accommodate motorized vehicles of the sort found in the Gobi. The only thing that denoted them as roads were some sticks laid on the ground indicating that, at some point, people decided that traffic should stay within the sticks. I live in a city with some of the oldest, most nonsensical roads in America, but Boston roads have *nothing* on these.

They crisscrossed and snaked across the village, forming loosely distinguishable blocks. The buildings were fairly uniform in their drab grey/tan, and covered in dust. The only exception to this was the school, which was painted an array of faded pastels, and was about the size of a convenience store. We piled out of the van and stared at our hotel, the tallest building in town at three stories. It had a "courtyard", which was gravelly earth separated from the rest of the town by a rusted tin fence. The courtyard was guarded by an angry grey-and-black tiger-striped tomcat and contained some rusted-out industrial equipment, a long drop toilet, and a massive tire laying on its side and sunken into the earth so only about 10 inches stuck out aboveground. Batzorig saw us looking at the tire and said, "It's to pee in. For men. You stand near it and pee."

"What's the long drop for then?" I asked.

"To shit," replied Batzorig. "You don't want to spend

any more time than you have to in there. Laura, you can pee anywhere, you don't have to use the tire," he said, then smiled, like this must have been a relief for her.

"Anywhere I want?" Laura asked, with a mock enthusiastic grin.

"Yes, anywhere. Women can pee wherever they want to. It's nice."

Our hotel, it turned out, besides being the only one in town, was also the only restaurant, bank, and convenience store. It did not, however, have bathrooms, running water, or real mattresses. The "beds" were wooden platforms with greasy-feeling blankets, and bedbugs as a special bonus. It was too hot to really need blankets, so we all piled the blankets in the corners of the rooms, put the bedrolls we generally traveled with on the platforms, and used some of our extra clothes as pillows.

Our first day in town was the Naadam festival and the village was soon full of nomads from all over this region of the Gobi. The off-road trucks, dirt-bikes, and horses seemed to just appear on the edges of town, converging on it from all directions. Batzorig was correct, there was a lot of mare's milk at Naadam. Custom dictated that each family bring a five-gallon aluminum saucepot filled with it, and they were all happy to share. He was also right about its taste. Not the delicious bit – but it being warm, salty, and bitter. It was terrible. Just awful. Imagine gamey milk that tastes like it's just gone bad, mixed with a touch of cheap vodka and salt, and served slightly warmer than room temperature. I choked down three or four glasses, hoping my disgust didn't show to the kind people who offered it to me. I was also presented with goat knuckles and a half-eaten sheep spine. The giant Mongolian man who offered it to me, after taking a slurping bite himself – maybe to show me how good it was? – was stone-faced, but lit up once I dug in with gusto. He rubbed my shoulders and said, "You eat like us! Goooood!" It was actually delicious, and the back rub was a nice touch.

I used to be a vegetarian. When I was around three years old, my sister convinced me that our parents fed us dog meat and told us it was chicken, beef, etc. This, oddly, did not make me feel any differently about my parents, but it did make me refuse to eat meat for long enough that it became habit. I grew out of it eventually, but dabbled in vegetarianism up until I was about 25, when I finally accepted that millions of years of evolution had made me an obligate omnivore. My longest stretch as a veggie was about six years. I was interested in Buddhism, and one of the teachings was to give up something, anything, that you don't really need. I gave up meat. Unfortunately, towards the end of the six years, it turned out I did need it. I was working 60+ hour weeks at my day job (which was really a night job) at a microbiology biotech lab, and filming, writing, editing, and researching my own webshow for about another 40 – this didn't leave time to devote to balanced meals. I was actually getting pretty sick and acting a little crazy. Perhaps sleeping less than five hours a night had something to do with it as well, but, my doctor said, "Some people can be vegetarians and be very healthy; you are not one of those people. I'm writing you a prescription for a chicken sandwich." I slowly rejoined the meat-eating community.

Even at the peak of my vegetarianism I would have never refused a lovingly prepared meal. If I went to a friend's house who didn't know I was vegetarian and they had spent a few hours making pork loin, I would eat it and deal with the intestinal upheaval later – hopefully long after I left their house. Brendan was that kind of vegetarian as well. He was our extraordinarily talented cameraman on the Brazil and Mongolia shoots. Brendan is a well-known high-fashion photographer and the cameraman for nearly every episode of *Austin Stevens: Snakemaster* and quite a few episodes of *River Monsters*. In any given week he can go from shooting nude supermodels having a glitter fight in London (true story) to filming an extremely dirty young man catching snakes in a distant jungle, both in 3D! He's South African, was arrested for protesting against Apartheid, and has lived everywhere including Pakistan (which he says is gorgeous) and Afghanistan. Brendan is talented and worldly enough that he would be able to get away with being extremely pretentious, but he isn't. He's quiet, a little goofy, thoughtful, and someone who is just interesting to talk to, about anything. His favorite topics are cinematography (which he can really geek out on a par with my biology nerd-dom), wildlife, and his kids.

Being a reformed vegetarian, Brendan and I had quite a few conversations about how interesting it was that most people don't consider fish animals. I don't understand, we would say. It's not like there are plants, animals, and fish. But very often you hear people say, "I'm a vegetarian, oh but I eat fish of course." This was not just a Western idea, either. In Mongolia, our fixer found out about Brendan's unfortunate "disorder": "But you eat pig right? Just not cow. Oh, goat? Lamb? Chicken? You must eat chicken? No? Woooow. Okay, we will have fish then." Brendan being Brendan, he would eat the dusty, expired tin of sardines that was produced for him while the rest of us gnawed on our camel steaks or goat bones. (Mongolia is not known for its cuisine.) This became such a frequent occurrence – the dusty tin of sardines produced for "poor Brendan, because of his problem" – that each time it would appear, the rest of us would start meowing and licking the backs of our hands then rubbing our faces, cat-like. Batzorig thought it was hysterical and got into it as well, proudly stating, "Brendan will have cat food please, he has problems," whenever we were given an option of different foods at restaurants or gracious people's homes.

In my experience, Mississippi has similar thoughts on vegetarianism. I was visiting my good friend Zeb, a marine biologist, down in MS one summer when I decided to have my first Sonic fast-food experience. I was amazed by the sheer number of choices – from drinks to sandwich options, I was overwhelmed. I decided to keep it simple, and asked the server, "Egg and cheese breakfast sandwich please."

"Bacon, sausage, turkey sausage, ham, or steak?"

"None, please, just egg and cheese."

"... I don't understand. Which meat?"

"That's okay, no meat please."

"It's fine, they all cost the same, you can pick whichever one."

"That's okay, I'll pay the same as if it had meat, but I don't eat meat."

"Oh, I'm sorry, I didn't, realize..." she said, like someone had just told the nice girl they had cancer or an embarrassing STD.

"No worries at all, not a problem," I assured her.

When my breakfast sandwich came out, it had chicken on it. The very smiley young girl who brought it to me (on roller skates) said, "Here you go! No meat, just like you asked. Usually we don't serve chicken this early in the day, but I did it special, just for you!" and she winked. I simply thanked her, and enjoyed an odd flavor combination.

The lack of running water in our hotel did make me a little nervous about the food we were eating, the plates we were eating it on, and the cleanliness of the hands of the folks who were preparing it, but Batzorig assured us that they used, "clean water that is brought in" – from where was never explained. A couple days into the excursion I noticed that the hoisin sauce I was slathering on my rice had expired six years before, and suddenly all things "cuisine" were put into perspective. I stopped worrying and dug in with gusto to our camel meat, unrefrigerated bacon left out in 100+ degree weather, oddly fermented beverages and "milkshakes" which were served with nearly every restaurant meal. This did lead to a few very unpleasant trips to the long drop.

I had mastered the "long-drop squat" in Cameroon, and was pleased to find that the one outside of our hotel actually had four walls around it. In fact, it was luxurious compared to most I had used. It was large enough that you'd have to stretch your arms to touch the sides rather than the normal "my shoulders barely fit in here" size. It had a wooden stabilizing bar for you to hold when you squatted, and the floor was not dirt, which far too easily hides other people's bad aiming or unfortunate explosive incidents. The first experience was not entirely unpleasant. The floorboards were a bit too spongy to really feel safe, and the walls, while present, were not without cracks and holes, allowing you a view while doing your business, and others a view *of* you doing your business. But, otherwise, it wasn't bad at all. The first time I used it was about 45 seconds after we arrived, before Naadam.

After a few hundred nomads had consumed excessive amounts of fermented mare's milk and hundreds of pounds of undercooked goat, that lone long drop saw more nomad butts than a very niche porn. After my blistering wrestling defeat I partook in a few fermented beverages and sampled some unsavory meat products myself. My stomach behaved admirably until about 2am, when I woke up sweating, realizing I had seconds to get to where I needed to go. Shaking, I put on a headlamp, ran downstairs, out into the courtyard, and threw open what appeared to be the gates of Hell. The once luxurious long drop had been transformed into a scene from a horror movie. There was shit, everywhere, mixed with other bodily fluids dripping from... oh, God, from the ceiling. "What had people *done* in here?" I thought, desperately. My stomach gurgled as I realized the time for contemplating what depravities had occurred in this tiny room could wait. I took my last breath of fresh air and stepped in.

The smell was like nothing before or since. It was what I'd imagine jumping into a pool of ammonia would smell like, if there was an undercurrent of feces and blood. The ammonia knocked me back figuratively, but the floor did it literally. The floorboards had felt a bit rotted before, but had been dry and given the impression of sturdiness. They now had a slick of human waste covering them, and each step brought liquids squelching to their surface, as if I was walking on a saturated sponge. My footfalls seemed to sink in and threaten to break through with each step, and the horror waiting 10 feet below was visible between each crack.

I nearly threw up, but was committed to this. I was not going to defile the pissing tire, which miraculously appeared to be pristine. Shaking, from fear and the desperate need to relieve myself of expired foodstuffs, I unbuckled my belt, assumed the position, and added to the corruption of this once-glorious toilet. I would not have touched the stabilizing bar for a month's salary, so I balanced, tentatively, over the wide opening. The ammonia smell burned all of my mucus membranes and made my eyes water to the point it was hard to see, but I managed to get my roll of "camper's tissue" out of my cargo pants and, after what seemed like hours – but was actually maybe three minutes – made my way cautiously out of the pit of despair.

Although I hadn't touched anything, I used nearly an entire bottle of hand sanitizer and a pack of antibacterial wipes. I didn't feel clean for days. The Gobi long drop became the stuff of legends with our crew. All of us braved it once before deciding to do our morning rituals in the open desert. The wind would whip up and sting your sensitive bits with blowing sand, used toilet paper would get caught by a breeze before you could bury it and you'd watch in horror as it flew 10 feet away, only to make a 180 degree turn and head straight at your chest – it was hard to dodge it when your pants were around your ankles. Yet, these hazards were infinitely preferable to reexperiencing the horror of that long drop.

Back on the road a couple days later, the long drop was a hot topic of conversation.

"Man, I don't even feel good about the bottoms of my shoes having touched that. I feel like I absorbed some disease through them," said James.

"It's been two days, and I think I can still smell it. Like, it's stuck in my nose or something," added Brendan.

"It's definitely permeated this shirt," I noted as I smelled my uniform shirt and winced. "God, how can it still smell?"

"Can you boys please stop talking about the smell of shit and piss for *five* minutes? I went in there once, because none of you warned me. You all waited outside giggling," said Laura. (This was true, and her reaction did *not* disappoint. A retching, "Oh no. *Blagh.* Oh fuck. Oh no. *Blach.* Oh fuck this. *Bloch.*" She came running out while we high-fived and laughed.) "It was fucking horrible, but it's over and done, and behind us. Now can we *please* focus on the task —"

James, who didn't seem to be listening, cut her off. "If that's the only long drop for a while, and the only running water is at the public bathhouse —"

"Shower. Public Shower," corrected Batzorig.

"Right, public shower. Then where does everyone..."

"I'm going to stop you right there," Laura cut in. "I'm sure this would have been a wonderfully pleasant and nuanced discussion about water shortages and..."

"Nope, I was going to say..."

"Oh, we all know what you were going to say, James, and I'd rather ... just not. I'd rather not right now. It's remarkable how your mind works, James. Jen's a lucky lady," said Laura.

Laura said, "Well, I'm glad we got that settled. Jesus Christ, 30 bloody minutes on long drops, you really are a bunch of regular Horatios, aren't you? Can we get back to discussing what we need to film today? Pat, you'll be happy to hear we'll be working with animals after we interview an eyewitness."

"Nice! Anything I should be prepared for?"

"Nah, they aren't very dangerous, just camels. You're going to ride one and talk about the legends of camels stepping on the Death Worm and then it exploding."

James smiled an evil smile. "So, we're going to have to do a re-enactment of a camel stepping on something right?"

"Well, I imagine we'll just film the camel's walking then CGI in a death worm and the explosion," Laura replied, without looking up.

Our first album would be *Deep Worker* in honor of the three-man sub we'd taken to the bottom of an oceanic trench in Canada.

"Don't think I didn't pick up on that smirk, James, and know exactly where that mind of yours is going," scolded Laura, although she was laughing, too. "I will not feed into this filth. It is time to focus, time to get your heads back on straight, you animals."

We arrived at the nomads' ger in the late morning and began discussing the most disgusting foods we'd ever eaten and the effects they'd had on our bodies as we piled out of the car.

Laura pleaded with us to focus and prepare for our next interview, which was with a man who allegedly saw a Death Worm while leading a group of Russian soldiers through the Gobi in the 1970s. I had read the account and it was bizarre but interesting. He saw the animal, and for some inexplicable reason the Russian soldiers he was guiding decided to pour gasoline on it, at which point it exploded and took the soldiers out. We ended the debate over the artistic direction of our fictitious band for the moment and started talking strategy for the interview while I got mic'd up. Brendan tested the camera while James did the same for sound and our producer scribbled notes for shots – basically, we all started doing our respective jobs.

Batzorig went ahead to speak with the witness and came back a few minutes later with some unexpected news. "So, this is not the witness. He is dead. They also have something for you to eat." These statements were said with the same matter-of-fact nonchalance, despite incredibly different implications for the shoot and the people involved.

"That's very nice that they have food for us, but our witness is dead?" said an equal parts concerned and confused Laura.

"Yes, he died many years ago. There was confusion with their names. We are meeting his very good friend. His wife has food and drinks for you and he will tell you his friend's story."

Well, a secondhand story was not as good as a first-person account, but was better than nothing. We went into the ger and began the traditional greeting. Batzorig had reviewed all of the "dos" and "don'ts" of entering a family's ger multiple times, but we thick Westerners were struggling. Each person needed to be greeted by shaking hands, but you needed to go counterclockwise – or was it clockwise? We all knew it wasn't through the middle – walking through the middle of a ger was tantamount to declaring your intention to break up the homeowner's marriage. We also knew we were supposed to accept any food or drink offered, and there was a way to accept it that none of us could completely get right, something with how you hold your hands. With enough smiles and apologies, however, and by avoiding the big no-no's, Batzorig thought we'd be okay.

The nomads had been more than willing to cut us slack, understanding that these customs were not our own and that we were trying. There would be laughs, jokes, hands shaken out of order, awkward hugs, and then food and drinks would be produced. Usually it was a bowl of sweets – candy from China, unusual homemade confections, or, once, M&Ms. It was polite to take one piece each time the bowl was handed to you and nod a thanks to the host. There would also be drinks – generally some delicious tea, or maybe a bottle of spring water. This pattern was well established in our minds – sweets, tea, thank-yous, interview.

We walked into the ger, deeper into the Gobi than we had yet ventured, and started our awkward greetings as Batzorig apologized for us and shook his head laughing. The bowl of sweets was produced and James, perpetually hungry, exclaimed, "Oh good, fudge!", and grabbed the largest chunk of what looked like delicious homemade penuche fudge. He popped the entire thing in his mouth as he passed the bowl. Laura took a decidedly smaller piece and started to nibble as we all heard James cough.

"Don't eat the fudge," was all he could choke out as his eyes watered and he looked for a drink.

The concerned nomads poured him a warm cup of mare's milk and added some salt – just the thing to wash down some sweets. None of us liked mare's milk, but we had all resigned ourselves to drinking it whenever it was presented, to be polite. We normally took a swig just as the bowl of sweets was coming back, and that way could kill the taste with a candy. James, we all noticed, didn't realize it was mare's milk in his distressed state and swigged a giant gulp, which did not help his predicament. He sputtered and coughed and gagged all at once.

"Oh, he must have bitten it," said Batzorig.

"The fudge?" I asked.

"Not fudge, mate, not fudge," said a slowly recovering James.

"What is fudge? This is curd!" said an excited Batzorig. "Homemade curd. It's very hard and delicious. Herders suck on it for hours and it lasts! It has a very strong, very delicious flavor."

It looked like James might disagree with this assessment, but our kind hosts were laughing. Apparently, anyone reacts that way after biting off a big chunk of curd – even those who inexplicably love the intense flavor. Laura was looking a little green but keeping hers down nobly, even smiling and nodding, and said, "Very good, thank you," while choking back tears. The bowl was passed to me and I had no option but to take a sizeable piece as all of the smaller ones had gone to Laura, Brendan, and our driver. I smiled, nodded, and thanked our hosts who watched anxiously as I put it in my mouth. It was a complex flavor – sour, acidic... vomit-like. The first note was definitely vomit, and was clearly causing the watering eyes. "Good God, I have no idea how James didn't puke," was my thought, as the undertones of sheep poo, camel spit, and possibly urine came to the surface. My piece was about half the size of James'. I decided to venture a sip of the fermented milk which had been poured for me. The flavors combined and somehow intensified each other. This was going to be a tricky one to get through.

"And it lasts for a very long time! Delicious, yes?" asked an enthusiastic Batzorig.

"Oh yes, thank you so much," we all managed. "Really good, very unusual."

"I can honestly say I've never tasted anything quite like this," Brendan managed.

James was laughing having now swallowed the remainder of his chewed curd like the bitter pill it was. "That caught me off guard! Delicious. Oh, I'm fine, yes, thank you, that was wonderful! No, no more for me, thanks. Very full. Should we get to filming? Who are we interviewing? Sir, could I please reach up your shirt to place a microphone somewhere?"

As soon as the hosts turned their attention to James, we simultaneously spat our remaining curd into our hands and pocketed it. Batzorig caught Brendan and looked shocked. He whispered, "You don't like it? It's delicious!"

I leaned in close to Batzorig and said, "We have very different definitions of that word, my friend. We'll talk later." He smiled, shook his head, and shrugged.

We were to interview the patriarch of this family, an

older man named Tarkhan. Tarkhan not only agreed to this interview, but also let us stay with his family and use his land as a basecamp of sorts for a few nights. While prepping for the interview, we were also setting up our own ger, unpacking our stuff, and claiming our sleeping spots. Tarkhan and his family looked on with bemused fascination. Tarkhan's little grandkids ran around playing with a mix of hand-carved and plastic toys while he watched and smiled. He had an incredibly friendly face – deeply lined, tanned, and loaded with smile wrinkles around his eyes and mouth. He was square-jawed and very handsome – he looked like he could have been a model in his younger days, with high cheekbones and dark hair. Even now, in his seventies, he retained the strong, defined physique that you could tell was a hallmark of his youth. He radiated warmth and kindness and seemed to always be smiling and laughing. His son, Bolt, looked a little like Yao Ming. He was enormous, at least 6'5", and very broad-shouldered. He had an angular face with a nose that appeared to have been broken a couple times, rippling muscles, and his hands were easily double the size of mine. At one point he picked me up like I was a kid and just laughed, a deep, resonating, baritone sound. It was no surprise when his proud father told us he was a champion wrestler. Bolt, ever modest, blushed and corrected Tarkhan, saying he wasn't a champion – he had just never lost a match.

Having introduced Bolt, I feel obliged to mention the odd names we came across in Mongolia at this point. I found that there is a tradition of naming children horrible or misogynistic things in an effort to fool evil spirits into thinking they were already cursed enough and thus leaving them alone. It wasn't uncommon to meet a very pretty young woman whose name translated into "pox girl", "dog", or "next time a boy". A few young men were named "donkey", "girl", "nobody", or "I don't know". There were even a couple people named Khünbish, which translates to "not a human". We don't even have a word for that in English. So all of the Dweezles, Apples, and Khaleesies of the world – take heart in knowing that at least your name isn't "not a human". Also, if your name is "Alan", you may want to choose a nickname on your next jaunt through Mongolia, as *your* name translates to "I will kill you".

Once mic'd up and ready for the interview I was formally introduced to Tarkhan. He smiled widely and shook my hand with gusto. We shared pleasantries through Batzorig's translation, and then I started asking about the death worm.

"Tarkhan, I understand that a very close friend of yours saw a creature that we call the Mongolian Death Worm many years ago. Can you tell me about what happened?" I asked with as much sincerity as I could. The story sounded outrageous to my biologist ears, but this guy was incredibly nice and earnest. He had no reason to lie to me and I decided right away to give him the benefit of the doubt and hear what he had to say.

"Yes, my good friend Nutzack many years ago saw the creature you are asking about," replied Tarkhan in earnest.

"I'm sorry, what did you say his name was?"

"Nutzak."

"Nutsack?" I asked, incredulously thinking maybe James had planned this.

"Yes, Nutzak."

At this point I noticed the camera shake slightly from Brendan's held-back laughter, and I could see that James had turned his face away. I shook my head, cleared my throat, and said, "Please tell me what happened to Nutzak," and we all tried our best not to de-evolve into 12-year-olds.

Once we finished the interview, thanked Tarkhan, and left for the next phase — the camels — Batzorig joined us near the car and asked, "Nutzak is not a common name, but it is not uncommon either. Why is this funny?"

Batzorig chimed in and asked, "Nutzak is not a common name, but it is not uncommon either. Why is this funny?"

"Well, Batzorig," I started, sheepishly, "it sounds a lot like a vulgar English phrase, and we were being a little immature and laughing about it."

"Oh, I love learning English phrases! What is nutzak?"

At this, even Laura chuckled. "Go ahead then, tell him," she said.

"It sounds a lot like 'nut sack', Batzorig, and 'nut sack' is a crude way of describing one's testicles," said James.

"Testicles?" asked Batzorig. "What are testicles?"

"Um, like a man's testicles, you know?" said an awkward Brendan, while making a cupping hand gesture.

Batzorig mimicked the gesture and said, ponderingly, "Test-i-culls?"

"Wow," I chimed in. "Yes, Batzorig, a man has testicles, and they are contained in a sac, the scrotum. We call testicles 'nuts', and sometimes the scrotum is called a 'sac' – nut sack, you see?"

He still looked confused, then started laughing. "Hahahha, I got you again! Yes, I know what testicles are! I wanted to see you explain them! Hahahhaha. Nut sack is new for me. It's like skin-bag, yes?"

"Yes, Batzorig, just like skin-bag. And good one, you did get us," admitted Laura.

We arrived at the camel herder's location after a couple hours of horribly immature conversation and seemingly directionless driving. To this day I have no idea how our guides navigated. I am not exaggerating when I say there were no tracks, no signs, no discernable landmarks – nothing to distinguish one spot from the next. I am not the best person to talk to about directions, but even James, who can navigate practically anywhere while driving any vehicle on any portion of road, was impressed. Somehow, these guys just knew where to go – maybe in this case they followed their noses.

The first thing I noticed about the camels was how bad they smelled. It was a sour, body-odor type smell, and really made me a little nauseous. I was embarrassed at first until I saw James gagging and Laura's eyes watering.

"Ripe old beasties, aren't they?" asked Rupert.

They weren't in very good moods either. While Brendan was setting up the camera, one spat on James. When you hear about a camel spitting it sounds funny, like a dog drooling on you, or a kid spitting a fountain of water. In real life, it is absolutely revolting. The camel is not spitting saliva, but is instead soaking you in its partially digested stomach contents that it regurgitates. It's closer to vomit than spit – thick, gooey, green, and smelling worse than the animals themselves. After hitting James, they laid a good one on me. They also shit constantly. It was just pouring out of their gaping buttholes, which were enormous. You couldn't help but walk in it – Brendan had to lay in it to get the close-up shots of the camel walking. Everything that came out of the camels smelled horribly. We all got spat and pissed on – they would wait until you were within splash distance to piss, and James and Brendan both got hit with all three excretions while getting extreme close-up shots.

"No wonder they're in such a bad mood," James remarked after the fourth camel vomited on him. "Did you notice the ticks?"

I had, in fact, noticed the ticks; they were hard to miss as the camels were covered in them. These were giant ticks, each a massive, blood-engorged parasite about the size of a large bon-bon – a blood-filled, living, repulsive bon-bon. They were the color of rotting skin – a dull, waterlogged grey, and seemed to congregate on the camels' chests, asses, and crotches. Especially their crotches. Dozens of these fetid-looking creatures feasted on each beast's genitals. It was awful.

"I'd be pretty angry if I had ticks all over my nether regions too. Especially *those* ticks," stated James.

When we finally finished with the camels we climbed back into the car, our collective odors melding together to rival the infamous long drop, and Brendan said, "That was far less fun than I thought it was going to be." We started the ride the ride back with a horrible game of "would you rather", initiated by Brendan asking, "Would you rather get spit on by a camel, or have to use that long drop?", which quickly made its way to, "Would you rather eat a tick from off the camels' crotches – not using your hands – or eat a four-course meal prepared by an amazing chef in the long drop." Answers were hotly debated by all in the car, although Laura made retching noises before answering and then posing her own scenarios.

Upon arriving back at camp, Laura informed us that we should take a nap because she had planned a night shoot once it was dark enough. Sleep is a rare commodity on shoots, and everyone tries to grab a little whenever possible. Normally, we would sleep in the car between locations, but between the otherworldly scenery, lack of roads, and constant threat of danger from the spark-emitting dashboard mixed with the ever present smell of gas, we were on alert in the Gobi-trekking vehicles. Naps were crucial whenever a night shoot was planned. I cannot nap though. I can fall asleep anywhere anytime – if you give me 15 minutes, I can be fully asleep. There could be a reenactment of the gang fight from the *Bad* video happening in front of me and I could still sleep in that weird parking garage. Problem is, once I'm asleep I need to either wake up in less than 30 minutes or stay asleep for more than three hours, otherwise I'm a mess.

A two-hour power nap might be just what the rest of the crew needed after being shat on by camels, but not me. I chose to spend the time hanging out with Batzorig – and by "hanging out", I mean drinking. The night shoot was going to be us making, and then consuming, homemade vodka, so I figured getting an early start couldn't hurt things. I have a great relationship with alcohol. I am neither an alcoholic nor a teetotaler. I don't drink very often and I believe myself to be a "fun" drunk. I tend to get happier than normal, pronounce my love for any casual acquaintance, and tackle people/try to ride on their backs. All in all, the photo and video evidence of my infrequent benders look like the people around me are all having a good time.

My mother is Italian and had the mindset that alcohol is like sugary cereal – not good for you, but not off limits to anyone in our house. This meant that we could always have a glass of wine at dinner, my sister's and mine being watered down, with the ratios shifting as we aged. Starting at about age nine we would get nips in our stockings at Christmas – just a tiny bottle of Kahlua or Grand Marnier, nothing you could get drunk on if you tried. At some point in the winter we would use it to make hot chocolate or milkshakes, or have it over ice cream, the three of us splitting one tiny bottle between us. My father has a hard time making subtle distinctions in life in general, and one year, when my mom asked him to grab the nips for our stockings, we received tiny bottles of Jack Daniels, Smirnoff, and test-tube shots. Mom was horrified and vowed that Al would never again do the Christmas shopping alone. To this day he will defend his actions with "booze is booze". Al was a beer brewer, and my reward for spending days helping clean and sterilize bottles, crush grains, pick and dry hops, etc. was either $5 cash or a bottle of beer. I always went for the beer, then casually dumped three-quarters of it. This all led to my not thinking of alcohol as a big deal and never getting into the "hide in the cemetery and drink" scene in high school, or going crazy in college.

In the middle of the Gobi Desert, however, when most people were asleep, a little vodka seemed like just the pick-me-up I needed.

Batzorig had other plans, though. "Here, I think you will like this," he said, producing a smallish glass bottle and puffing his chest out as he set it in front of me.

"Woah, snake wine," I said in awe as I grabbed the bottle. It looked like a homemade, fat-bottomed, half-liter bottle with a murky, sediment-laden liquid and a sizeable rat snake filling it. An entire snake.

Batzorig poured two shots, and he and I then recited our favorite toast, which was Mongolian for "bottom's up and get drunk", but sounding to our Western ears like "top toy, sock toy". James had started doing hand gestures that went along with the words. We drank quite a bit in Mongolia and this had become ritual. While saying "top toy" you would give the thumbs up and pretend to play with something, followed by "sock toy" while miming a hand puppet. Batzorig loved it, and adopted it himself.

Top-toy sock-toy indeed. The snake wine tasted a bit like old fish mixed with cheap vodka. Batzorig, a man with a much stronger stomach than I, said, "This is shit, yes? Blach!" I had to agree, it was shit. This didn't stop us from laughing at what surely lay ahead of us and each having another shot. There is a bizarre phenomenon where the taste of some alcohol improves after the first shot. This was not the case with snake wine. We decided it would be wrong of us to drink it all ourselves as the crew deserved to share in this experience, so we switched to a bottle of Chinggis vodka for a final shot, then both fell asleep where we sat in the oppressive heat of the Gobi afternoon.

We weren't asleep for long. After what seemed like five minutes I was woken by a frazzled-looking Laura standing over us, shouting, "Get up, get up, they've started the vodka." James, bleary-eyed, was rounding up all of the equipment and placing lapel mics on the confused-looking nomads. Without Batzorig to translate, James' miming of, "I'm going to stick something down your shirt," hadn't gone over too well, except for one older lady who seemed flattered. They had butchered a goat and chopped it into fist-sized pieces. The entrails were being devoured by a couple of the families' dogs, who up until that moment had seemed like the nicest, most placid and welcoming animals I had worked with in years. It was disturbing to see their friendly muzzles – muzzles that had snuggled our arms for hugs and scratches earlier in the day – covered in blood and gore.

I shook it off and saw Laura staring in horror. "It's probably best we didn't film the slaughter, eh?" We all nodded.

The goat pieces were placed in a giant metal pot half-filled with water and some herbs. I asked where they had gotten the water, but never received a response – it was another Gobi mystery that would go unsolved. Large rocks had been placed in a bonfire earlier in the day and were now being taken out and placed into the pot. Most people were using wooden tools to maneuver the super-heated stones, but Bolt, the toughest man on Earth, was using his bare hands. We stared in open-mouthed horror and heard his flesh sizzling. He saw us watching, laughed, mimed burnt hands blowing on his fingers and shook his hands comically, then laughed again and dropped a stone into the pot where it let out an audible "hiss". After a dozen-or-so rocks a pressure-cooker lid was sealed and we were told the meat would be ready around the same time as the vodka.

The process for making the vodka was much easier than I expected. There was no pressurized still involved and no risk of an explosion. When we entered the stifling hot ger, a few women and girls were in the process of pouring about five gallons of fermented mare, goat, and sheep milk into a pot that looked capable of holding about 20 gallons. They were also suspending a small metal bowl in the large pot by tying camel-hair rope around the handles of the inner and outer pots, making the small inner pot float about halfway between the surface of the milk and the top of the outer pot, dead center. I was told this inner pot would collect the vodka. The whole contraption was then placed on a grate over a very hot fire – the source of the extreme temperatures in the ger. A massive wok was placed on the outer pot, more than covering it, and water was poured in. I was told that as the fermented milk heated up the alcohol in it would boil off first and the vapors, upon contact with the relatively cool wok, would condense into fairly pure alcohol, run down the convex surface of the wok until they reached its apex, then drip into the collecting pot, which would be periodically emptied into a different vessel by people with hands like Bolt's. This worked remarkably well.

In order to make the strongest possible vodka, this process would normally go on for about two hours, then the resulting liquid would go through the same process two more times, meaning the leftover milk would be discarded and replaced with the first run of vodka, then the leftover water would be discarded, and you would end up with near lab-strength ethanol. Batzorig told me not many people had the patience or stomach for this, and tradition was to distill twice. As we were novices and assumed, correctly, to be both extraordinarily uncomfortable in the heat of the ger and lightweights when it came to drinking vodka, we went with only one distillation. After the process had yielded about a liter of clear, vaguely cheese-smelling liquid, we called it quits, much to the amusement of the unfazed, sweaty nomad women.

Having learned this vodka-making technique in Mongolia, I decided to try it at home with an off batch of cider I'd brewed in Massachusetts. That year, I made nearly the legal maximum of 200 gallons, and, it's safe to say, not every batch was a winner. It seems wrong to dump alcohol down the drain, especially alcohol you had pressed, seasoned, fermented, and bottled yourself, so I thought: "I did this in Mongolia while a little drunk and with next to no sleep; this should be easy!" I jury-rigged roughly the same setup and went about distilling 3 gallons of my worst product. After filling our new house with terrible odors of boiling spoiled cider, nearly destroying a few pots and pans, and burning all my fingers, I had managed to collect about a pint of "vodka". Before I could sample it, though, Anna asked a question. Being infinitely more detail-oriented, cautious, and levelheaded than I am, she wondered aloud: "It really doesn't matter what you start with? I mean, in Mongolia, you were starting with fermented mare's milk, and here, you're starting with cider, bad cider; I feel like that makes a difference." Hmmm ... maybe? A quick Google search showed that it does, in fact, matter what you start with, and cider has a naturally high methanol percentage that distilling the way I had done has a tendency to retain and concentrate. Mare's milk, on the other hand, has nearly no methanol and therefore poses no risk. Essentially, I had inadvertently, possibly, distilled a pint of poison. Google then told me that there was a pretty simple assay I could do to test for the presence of methanol, but, for better or worse (probably better), everyone around me had lost their faith in my chemistry skills, and it was agreed that my *eau de vie*, rather than consumed by humans, was best poured out for the Greenman as a sacrifice to ensure that next year's apple harvest would be a good one. My distilling career peaked in Mongolia, I'm afraid.

Bolt checked the goat by reaching into the pot and pulling out a bone with some meat clinging to it, taking a huge bite that seemed to steam in his mouth, and giving us the "thumbs up", using a thumb that must have been made of stone or asbestos. The meat was done, the vodka was done (it would be served hot – not warm, hot), and we were ready to start the feast. This particular manner of feast, called a khorkhog, is reserved for special occasions, like when guests visit from far away, and there are certain customs that go with it. Most of these traditions required extremely heat-resistant hands. One custom was to remove the hot rocks from the stew and pass them around, with each diner tossing them from hand to hand and then to the next person in a bizarre game of "hot potato" that had no winner or loser. The rock simply went down the line, then was tossed to the dogs, who anxiously licked them to suck out all of the fat they had accumulated while cooking. The next stone then repeated this process until there were only four stones left. The stones were placed on the tray with the meat to keep them warm. This tray was passed around and we all grabbed chunks of delicious, tender, fall-off-the-bone goat.

Another tradition was passing the metal bowl of hot vodka. You had to hold the bowl with all of your fingers, and it was considered immature to move your fingers around to prevent them from getting burned – not immature like burping at the table, but rather like "only kids need to do this" – kids and Westerners. All of us did this, and got a lot of laughs.

"Holy Hell that's hot," was James' reaction when it was passed to him, and he commenced blowing on his fingers to everyone's amusement. Bolt showed us how it was done by cupping the entire thing in his massive hands and making unbroken eye contact with each of us for 30 seconds. It was both impressive and intimidating.

Next came the first sip of vodka, which custom dictated was preceded by dipping your ring finger in it and flicking it in the air three times, then, on the fourth dip, touching your forehead. This is done very slowly and deliberately, and means:

I hope for the health of everyone,
I hope for good weather and rain for the crops,
I hope for everyone to be at peace, and for the world to be at peace,

And finally –

Thank you for this vodka, and I hope for my own health.

Only then can you take a sip and pass it on to someone else of your choosing. The order of drinkers would normally have significance as well, but we Westerners were forgiven this custom because we were told "it's very confusing" – as opposed to the rest of it, which was so straightforward.

Tarkhan started us off, dipping, flicking, and touching his forehead. The ritual was fascinating and quite moving. The respect was palpable and we all loved what it stood for. After taking his sip, he made a toast.

"Welcome to Mongolia, honored guests! We are so happy to have you here, and so glad that you've agreed to share in this traditional meal in the traditional manner. Our customs must seem strange, but you have participated and accepted them without question. You have shown us great respect, and we have enjoyed talking with you and sharing our culture. Filming is your job and your love, but your families and health come first. I hope you finish filming very well and find everything you want, but more than that I hope you find happiness and return home to your family safe and healthy. Now, I hear there is another custom Batzorig has filled you in on. I'd like to continue it. TOP TOY SOCK TOY!" And he mimed our hand gestures. We all laughed, and the feast started in earnest.

We found that no one else was expected to give a toast, but everyone was expected to sing a song after taking their sip before passing the bowl to the next person. Tarkhan passed the bowl to Bolt, who sang a rousing anthem-like military song in a deep baritone. We all applauded and drank the vodka that had been poured for us. Bolt passed to me. I thanked him, took a sip – noticed that it tasted like hot parmesan, which is not nearly as unpleasant as it sounds, and sang *Boys on the Docks* by the Dropkick Murphys, telling the assembled group it was an "important song about family and friends from my town, Boston." I forgot a few words, but everyone clapped with gusto. I passed to James, who sang the national anthem of Wales, in Welsh. He passed to Bolt's oldest daughter who sang an absolutely beautiful song about lost love. She passed to Laura who sang something by Babyshambles, and so the night went

– drinking and drinking and unaccompanied renditions of our favorite songs. Eventually, we all sang along to help each other out and picked songs like *Lovely Rita* which we would all know the words to – the nomads did the same, and we cheered and laughed, going from nomad, to Brit, to nomad.

At some point, Bolt suggested we add dried goya to the vodka. "Isn't that toxic?" I asked.

He laughed. "Yes, but it's delicious!" He added a bit and it gave it a very earthy undertone which improved the already unique and tasty cheese flavor.

We did a few more Beatles tunes, a few Clash, a couple Ramones, Queen, and *Total Eclipse of the Heart*. Then things started getting weird. With Batzorig's encouragement, I did an impression of Meatwad from *Aqua Teen Hunger Force* singing *One Step Closer* by Linkin Park before we moved on to nursery rhymes, and eventually (what we would later find out to be) offensive, ribald drinking songs from our hosts, and sea shanties from our crew. The first couple were tame enough and elicited groans from those of us not singing, but the same enthusiastic applause from the nomads who didn't understand the words, but loved James' voice particularly. After the third, his songs became their favorites – he knew every word (unlike the rest of us, who would devolve into drunken laughter at the first mistake in a verse), and his voice really was very good! Their clear enjoyment and encouragement emboldened him to get more and more crass, moving from the risqué and slightly off-color to implicitly filthy limericks put to music. James would later say he went from "bawdy" to "straight-up filthy" really quick.

After one particularly raucous number, Laura started shooting him her best mom looks, which unequivocally said, "Watch yourself, young man!" But he had the crowd, and he knew it, and the fact they were *loving* it only made him up the ante quicker. He went on to some old-timey-sailor drinking songs, followed by an old tune where James taught the room the chorus and instructed us all how to keep the beat by alternately slapping our legs and clapping.

The song gets worse and worse, and ends with a non sequitur which is not fit for print, but was delivered in a glorious, rousing ringing baritone, holding the last note for more than 10 seconds. That, along with the singalong, and easy-to-pick-up chorus, left the kind Mongolians ecstatic, and they gave an uproarious salute. Not speaking a word of English, thank God, they just loved the tunes, James' showmanship, and his voice. The man really does have a great voice for super-offensive songs.

However, it was finally too much for Lady Laura, and the rest of us, even as drunk as we were. "JAMES! On that note, I am going to bed. You boys should too; this is getting. Out. Of. Control."

Giggling, we followed suit, hugging, high-fiving, and shaking hands with our wonderful hosts as we stood up to leave. Tarkhan made the final toast, saying how great we were and how pleased they were to meet us. He said they had found us to be nice, "not jerks or judgmental", and said, in closing, "You drink with us, eat goat in a traditional way, respect our customs, sing incredible songs, and DRINK! You are Mongolians too!" We all laughed, and cringed a bit at the "incredible songs" bit, then hugged and high-fived some more, before ducking out of the ger and heading up to our own.

On the way I spotted my first camel spider on the ground. Given that I was very, very drunk, I decided to chase it, yelling to James, "Hey! Hey, James, I'm chasing a camel!"

"Oh! Good for you, mate, have fun," he slurred.

"Spider, I mean, I'm chasing a... thing. A thing you should see, man. You should see this shit!" I shouted enthusiastically.

"I don't want any more camels, the dirty bastards. Spat all over me. The state of things they put me in!" said James as he stumbled a bit.

"What about camels now?" said a slurring Brendan.

"Pat's spotted one and is chasing it. I think there are spiders involved," said James, helpfully.

"Oi! Enough!" said an exasperated Laura.

"You both need to see this, I'm going to grab it!" I yelled.

Lady Laura sounded faint all of a sudden. "Pat, leave that bloody thing alone and get your arse back here!"

I looked up. Why was everyone so far away? How had I gotten all the way out here?

"But he's getting away!" I whined.

"I know, Pat, and that's hard right now, but you need to let him go. Don't wander off after strange animals again, okay?" she said, placating me.

"Isn't that the whole reason we're here?" I replied cheekily, as I jogged back towards the sound of her voice.

"He has a point, you know," Brendan said.

"Don't be fresh, and don't encourage him. He'll be in the middle of the bloody desert if this keeps up. Oi! Pat! Don't chase animals tonight," she said, seeing me turning to go back after it. "No camels, spiders, goats, sheep, snakes, monkeys, death worms, orcs, or anything else. Go to bed!"

Laura's best mom-voice really worked. Something deep down told me she meant business, and I turned with my tail between my legs and said, "Sorry, Laura," sulking off to my spot in the ger. "But if I see a monkey, or an orc, I'm definitely going to chase it."

"Go to sleep, TV's Pat Spain," she replied, wearily.

The next morning, along with a killer hangover, I had an overwhelming feeling that we all needed to apologize – to someone, for something. This anxiety turned out to be unfounded. Our wonderful hosts greeted us looking distinctly better than any of our crew, and thanked us again, saying how incredible it was of us to throw ourselves into their traditions like we had. They were actually a bit cowed. Apparently some of their songs had been more risqué than we'd realized! Everyone around the world gets a little loose when the vodka flows. They kept shaking our hands and saying how brilliant it was, telling James what a great voice he had. James, looking a bit embarrassed in addition to very ill, apologized, saying he knew they couldn't understand the lyrics, but thought he'd gone a bit too far nonetheless. Luckily, our hosts disagreed and talked about James' "lovely songs" for the duration of our stay.

Laura did not agree with their assessment. "Yes, you were very naughty, James. Very, very naughty," she said. "Let's have no more of it. In fact, in light of the debacle last night, culminating in almost losing Pat, I'm calling a Lady's Day today. That means no one can talk about urination, defecation, genitals, intercourse, breaking wind, eating ticks, camel anatomy, disgusting foods, or any topic unbefitting of a Lady. Got it? You wankers?" asked Laura, killing the effect a bit at the end, but getting her point across.

"We have become disgusting animals, haven't we?" I asked, and cringed at the sound of my own voice.

"A bit, yeah," she replied. "But I love you all. It's just getting to be a bit much. Let's tone it down, yeah?"

We all nodded our agreement, muttering half-hearted apologies. All feeling a bit awful for putting Laura, who never drank on a shoot, in a position where she had to call us out in order to move the project forward. Just then Batzorig approached us having emerged from his ger, grinning. "Which of you nut sacks wants breakfast?" he yelled, as soon as he was within earshot.

Oh no. This was our fault. We had turned Batzorig, a gentle, kind, and smart man, into someone who called people "nut sacks" before breakfast. Shame washed over all of us as we silently resolved to clean ourselves up – for the day, at least.

Chapter 3

Fossils, Rabbits, and Nicolas Cage

Mongolia's tourism slogan is "Go Nomadic, Experience Mongolia", which is *fine*. Tourism slogans are, as a whole, fine. Some are better than others, such as "Djibouti: Djibeauty", "Travel in Slovakia – Good Idea", which sounds like a veiled threat or sarcasm, depending on your intonation, and "Think Hungary More than Expected", which raises so many questions, and definitely needs some punctuation. (Honorable mentions to "I Feel Like Tunisia" and "Live Your Unexpected Luxemburg", which both break the rule of "don't use the word in its definition".) So, compared to others, "Go Nomadic, Experience Mongolia" is pretty good. In my experience, though, it should be "Mongolia – Crazy Shit Around Every Corner!" I think that would drive up tourist numbers significantly.

If Mongolia were a person it would be Nicolas Cage. Everyone loves Nicolas Cage – I challenge you to not watch *National Treasure* if you are flipping through the channels and see it's playing. No one knows a whole lot of truths about Nicolas Cage, but we definitely know of him and his exploits – some of which are maybe untrue, but we still believe them because the ones we know to be true are so bizarre and awesome. It would take most of us a minute to point to Nicolas Cage on a map, even though he's a very, very big country – I mean, celebrity, very A-list, I think. Right? Nicolas Cage is also rife with fossils, more fossils than any other celebrity.[source needed] And crazy – Nicolas Cage is crazy. And so is Mongolia – in a wonderful and beautiful way. "BEEEEEEEEEEEEEEEEEEEEEEEEEES!!!!!"

Mongolia is enormous – the 18ᵗʰ largest country by land area, in fact, and the largest landlocked country that doesn't border a closed sea, which feels like too many qualifiers. It's like when a commercial says, "It's the number one comedy in America among 18-25-year-old men, who live alone... and have at least two cats." It is massive though, and very few people live there. It's the world's most sparsely populated country, and you can easily go weeks or months traveling within its borders without bumping into another person. But at the same time you can find people (and things) when you least expect to.

Batzorig woke us early one morning to tell us he'd had a call and a friend of his had found a snake. Would we like to see it? This was a pleasant surprise! The fact that we had only fallen asleep four hours before and were all a bit hungover (all but Laura, who smartly did not drink on shoots) was less pleasant. our producer quickly huddled to review the schedule and decided that it would just be another long day (18 hours) of filming, but this was worth it – we didn't know if we'd find another snake. It was a 2-3 hour drive to his friend's place, so we needed to get moving.

After a quick breakfast of unrefrigerated bacon, eggs, and condiments that had expired sometime in the previous decade we jumped in our perpetually smoking, sparking, and diesel-smelling car, wondering if this was the day it (or we) died. As it happens, it was the day the car died. After an hour or so delay where I picked flowers and pressed them in letters to Anna and my journal like a Victorian dandy, we pushed the car for a bit and got it rolling again. (Normally, I would say "back on the road", but as I've mentioned there were no roads where we were.)

There were no trails, no signposts, no real landmarks to speak of. Just varying degrees of "desert" – some scrub brush, some hilly, some sandy – in all directions. We trusted Batzorig and his crew to get us where we needed to go, and they always did. They didn't use a compass or any other instrument. Once, I saw the driver get out of the car and look up, walk around the car, look up again, look left, look right, think, drum on his face with his fingers, then jump back in and go in the same direction as before we'd stopped. I asked him why he'd done this and his reply was "fun" – but he was not smiling when he said it. He was definitely the strong and silent type.

At one point on the way to the snake we picked up a hitchhiker, just a Mongolian dude in jeans and a white polo standing in the middle of the desert, literally nothing around him in any direction, like he was placed there by a spaceship. He got in, said a few words to our driver, nodded to each of us, and we rode in silence for about an hour, at which point he got out – again, in the middle of the desert. The landscape didn't change, there was no bus stop, he didn't ring a bell, tap the driver's shoulder, or otherwise indicate that "this was the place". Our guy just stopped the car and the dude jumped out. James asked, hesitantly, if they knew each other. Batzorig laughed and the driver simply said, "No," and continued driving for another hour until we got to Batzorig's friend's place. It was amazing. Had we gone out of our way to drop off this rambler? Had we just driven him to the middle of nowhere to await certain death? None of us knew.

The snake was at a herder's temporary dwelling that seemed more permanent than the gers we'd been staying in. This had a few permanent structures on the land, one of which was a tool shed that allegedly contained the snake. It ended up being two good-sized rat snakes, but all the guides and herders insisted they were deadly vipers, which got me a little over-prepared and psyched up. I was able to catch them both and found that some thread had gotten wrapped around one's neck and somehow got into its throat. I was able to cut this off and remove it without injuring the animal and likely saved its life. Everyone clapped, which was a very cool reaction for saving a snake's life. We then had a nice visit with the lovely herder and his family, who offered us our daily dose of mare's milk.

We piled back in the car, the mare's milk mixing nicely

with our long-expired breakfast, and started the trip back to our home base. After an hour or two the driver suddenly sped up and started veering all over the place, like he was about to start doing donuts, then changed his mind and went in the other direction. All of us were concerned. He was laughing and smiling and yelled, "Rabbit! Dinner!" then slammed on the brakes and jumped out, shouting, "Come! Fun!"

We had all been dozing before, but were all very awake and confused now. I looked out the window and saw our 6′4″ driver laughing hysterically and grabbing huge rocks and hurling them with all of his strength at, apparently, a rabbit? None of us could see a rabbit, but he continued bellowing, "Come! Fun! Rabbit!"

I said, "I'm definitely not throwing rocks at a rabbit." Laura agreed, as did Brendan, our producer was on the fence, but James was in.

"Okay, mate, I'll help you get the bunny."

He jumped out, looked around, and said, "Guys, I really don't see any rabbit, but this is the happiest I have ever seen this man. I feel like we should throw some rocks with him." This didn't seem like the worst idea, so we did.

We piled out of the car and, laughing and sweating, threw rocks aimlessly for about 10 minutes. Just chucking them in any direction. The driver then said, "Ah! Missed him. Too bad. Next time eh? Fun!"

And it *was* fun, he was right. We did not have rabbit for dinner that night, we had egg noodles with mystery meat. We didn't actually see a rabbit at all. But we did throw a lot of rocks.

Next day was another long car trip in a seemingly random direction, but instead of ending up in a sketchy tool shed I found myself in what appeared to be Mars, but what was actually Nemegt – the land of dinosaurs.

It was surreal, a completely alien landscape. Red sandstone everywhere with weird shapes sticking out of it. We passed fossilized trees stabbing out of rocks, jutting up from the sand, and laying on the ground in piles. Actual fossils! Just laying around! We all forgot about filming for a while and reverted to childhood, when every kid went through a "fossil hunter" stage, only instead of finding indistinct patterns on rocks that my father would agree did "look like a small dinosaur footprint! How exciting!" we were finding actual fossilized shells, tons of them, along with plants, whole trees, ferns, other markings and more.

"Pat! Come over here in a moment, please! No one walk over here other than Pat. Brendan, please start filming. If this what I think, I want to get Pat's first reaction on tape."

Whenever I heard the phrase, "I want to get Pat's first reaction on tape," from the director, it either meant really good things for me, or really, really bad things. It meant, "There's an eyelash viper right at eye level in that tree, and I know you've always wanted to find one," or "There's a local delicacy that we *really* think you need to try. You may not feel... well afterwards, so it's the last thing we're filming today."

"HOLY SHIT!" I heard James exclaim, who had just had a talk with Laura.

"Yeah, 'holy shit' is right," said Laura. "Brendan, are you rolling? James, do we have sound? Okay, release Pat!"

"What am I looking for?" I said, hesitantly, still not knowing if this was going to be good or bad for me.

"Um, I dunno, you tell me. Genuinely – none of us are completely sure of what it is," came Laura's reply.

Anticipation building, I walked toward his voice, looking around. Vipers? Cool lizards? Giant insects? Oh – a, rock. Okay... I reached down and started to brush the rock off.

"Wait. Wait. HOLY SHIT! Yeah! HOLY SHIT! Is this a fucking dinosaur egg?"

"Well, that's the general reaction we were hoping for, but maybe a little less –"

"HOLY SHIT! There are more! Oh my GOD! Look at this! This is a... a nest! A fucking *nest* of dinosaur eggs!"

James and Brendan both forgot we were filming at that point and said, "No way, let me see! We only saw the one egg sticking up! Oh my GOD!"

"Well, we'll have to film this whole thing again with far less vulgarity, but, holy shit – yes, I think you're right. Look at that! And another one and – they just keep coming!" said an ecstatic Laura.

We'd found a nest of dinosaur eggs, recently uncovered by the shifting sands of the Gobi, just sitting there. A nest of dinosaur eggs, no mistaking it. None of us could believe it. We all held them, took pictures, and just basked in it – dinosaur eggs. Then we had a little moral dilemma. Clearly we all want to have a dinosaur egg on our mantle at home, but also clearly that is wrong and illegal, and the running theme was: "We don't want to do a dual episode of *Beast Hunter* and *Locked Up Abroad*." We asked Batzorig what the protocol was for something like this, and he said, "Can I keep one?" then laughed. Then asked, "Can I have one?" again.

We knew we wanted them to go to the museum we had visited in Ulaanbaatar, but didn't want to be found traveling with them. A week earlier, we'd been stopped and had our things searched, when the police turned up a few rocks I'd collected (I usually took a few leaves, a couple small rocks, and other little natural-history souvenirs from my trips) and decided they were "soil samples meant for the detection of minerals and natural resources", potentially a federal crime. A short conversation with Batzorig and some "fees" cleared this "misunderstanding" up, but it had left us very concerned about transporting anything that came from the ground.

We decided the safest course of action was to take a GPS pin of the location and let the museum know, which we did. The eggs were collected the following day, we were told, and that was the last time I thought about their eventual location until December 2015 when a news article caught my eye: "Nicolas Cage agrees to return stolen dinosaur skull to Mongolia." Who could not read that article?

It claimed that a Tyrannosaurus bataar skull "and other dinosaur artifacts" had been illegally smuggled out of Mongolia then sold by legit auction houses, with the skull eventually winding up with Nicolas Cage after he purchased it for $267,000 on a spending spree that would nearly bankrupt him. Once the true origin of the skull came to light, Nick agreed to give it back to Mongolia to have it displayed in the Natural History Museum where it belonged. The article then said that the US had recently recovered many illicit dinosaur artifacts from Mongolia, "including a nest of dinosaur eggs found in Nemegt in 2010".

I can't prove this, but it's very possible that my "1 degree of separation" from Nicolas Cage is a nest of illegally smuggled dinosaur eggs thanks to my trip looking for the Mongolian Death Worm.

Chapter 4

The Greatest Name in All of Cryptozoology – the Mongolian Death Worm

Hello there, and thank you for making it this far with me. We've come to the "cryptid" or mysterious animals that may or may not exist chapter of the book. This is either a very weird turn in the funny travel book you've been enjoying, or you've been *very* confused by the first few chapters of the cryptozoology book you purchased. I will not be citing my sources here (most of them are my own notes and memories anyway). Feel free to google anything I mention and write angry emails and nasty tweets about how I got the square mileage of the Gobi Desert wrong. This is not a paper in a scientific journal, it's a collection of true stories from my personal experiences, and some of my opinions. When making *Beast Hunter*, we needed to cite at least two credited (peer-reviewed or expert-opinion) sources for every fact I stated on camera. There was a factchecker at Nat Geo whose job was to pick apart every line. Most networks do not require this, but it's one of the reasons I love Nat Geo so much, and why Nat Geo is among the most respected brands in the world. This did mean our job of making films about animals that may or may not exist was very difficult. There were so many retakes in order to throw in a "perhaps" or a "some experts say" that we ended up doing a five-minute reel of me just repeating phrases that imply ambiguity in different intonations which we could cut in during editing. Realistically, we loved the scrutiny and I feel it made the series much better than your run-of-the-mill crypto show filled with statements like "that's definitely a werewolf" when someone hears a barred owl; or an episode with more night-vision footage than a wannabe actor's "break-out" video (regardless of whether the proposed animal is nocturnal or not) with lots of loud noises and Blair Witch-style nausea-inducing camera movements, followed by, "What's THAT?!?", or – in my opinion the biggest crime in this field – faked news stories or actors playing scientists. That is bullshit, I say!

There were a few things in *Beast Hunter* that were cut by our factchecker which I would still argue were true. We had to lose a whole segment when I caught a hagfish because I said, "They aren't closely related to anything else, and they really aren't even a fish by a strict definition." I *may* have slightly overstated how different they are evolutionarily, but I maintain that what I said was true. My friend Zeb, a marine biologist, is probably cringing reading this, but it's that kind of scrutiny and adherence to the truth that I think set our show apart. Anyway, there is no factchecker on this book, other than you, dear reader. So check away, but as I said, these are mostly my own thoughts, opinions, and experiences.

In case you haven't figured it out yet, I am a nerd. Not like, "Oh, I went to Comic-Con, I'm such a nerd" – a real nerd, and specifically a science nerd. This differs from the so-hot-right-now comic book/sci-fi nerd. Sure, I liked *Fringe* as much as the next guy, I've read all of the *Song of Ice and Fire* books to date, and my high-school friends and I stayed in on Friday nights to watch *The X-Files*, but my true nerd status really becomes apparent whenever a conversation strays into any topic in biology. I advocated for the name "Darwin" if our first child was a boy, and when we found out we were having a daughter I tried to convince Anna it would still make a great middle name. We ended up naming her Luna after the amazingly beautiful and mysterious *Actias luna*, the luna moth. Yes, I'm aware that Luna Lovegood is a character in one of my favorite book series – she's one of Anna's and my favorite characters, in fact, but that's an added bonus for the name rather than a driving force. Our son is named Wallace Charles after Alfred Russel Wallace, Charles Darwin, and Charles Fort.

I was a teaching assistant for multiple chemistry and biology labs and audited extra biology and philosophy classes – for fun. I traveled to Maryland to observe horseshoe crabs mating – again, for fun. One of the only real fights I can remember getting into with my best friend since birth was when we were eight and he insisted that crabs were amphibians. The only TV shows I watched in the eighties and nineties were nature programs. Whenever I was sick and off school I was allowed to rent anything I wanted from the video store. My pick was always a volume of *Life on Earth*. David Attenborough, Alfred Russel Wallace, and Charles Darwin were my childhood heroes, and remain my adult heroes – in addition to Harry Marshall, the founder and head of Icon Films and the man responsible for sending me on all of these adventures and forever changing the course of my life. He also makes damn fine TV.

When I left home at 16 and lived on my own for the first time it was for a marine biology internship in Maine. A friend asked what the nightlife was like in southern Maine. I replied, with no hesitation or sense of irony, "Great! It's really awesome! There are foxes, raccoons, lightning bugs, polyphemus moths, and so far I've spotted two species of owls!" I also read the *Fortean Times* and *CryptoZooNews*, and most of the people I follow on social media are naturalists. Don't worry, though – I won't get *too* scientific in this chapter (and there will be poop jokes).

I say all of this because in recent years there has been a move towards hijacking nerd culture by moderately cool people. An actor who can't quite cut it turns to fantasy shows and suddenly he's a heartthrob. A few years back, even Charlie Sheen "led a search for the Loch Ness Monster". I happened to be in Scotland investigating the same monster at the same time, and heard some horror stories from the locals about his behavior in their beautiful country. I am not a person who does this stuff for the attention. I do it because I love it, am fascinated by it, and think it doesn't do science any favors to simply write off things that sound bizarre.

Too many scientists forget that the general public does not consist primarily of other scientists, and most people would rather hear about the *possibility* of a bipedal intelligent ape walking around in the Great North Woods than the reality of the new barnacle you discovered. Run with that, talk about the *possibility*, it will get people listening. Make them things that people, real people, will find interesting, then talk about wolverines, the reintroduction of wolves, and pine martens. Throw in some jokes, give some sexy facts – more people would be interested in your barnacle if you led with the fact that it has the largest penis-to-body ratio of any animal in the world –it's over six times the total length of its body! That's CRAZY! And fascinating! And memorable. Where do they keep it? How do ... I'm getting sidetracked, the point is — don't refuse to talk about something because you think it sounds silly. Getting people outside for a homemade Bigfoot expedition still gets them outside, and they *will* see other amazing and exciting things even if they don't see a sasquatch. A generation of Bigfoot hunters might turn into conservationists, or field biologists, or maybe lawyers who want to protect the land they loved exploring as a kid. Another interesting side effect of not immediately writing these things off, all of you closed-minded scientists out there, is that sometimes, *sometimes*, you might find that there is actually *something* to these stories. If you go out there, use your scientific training, open your mind, dispel disbelief and really look at the facts and evidence you might surprise yourself, like I did with the Mapinguari in Brazil, and others.

I'm an open-minded skeptic at heart, and I approached everything around *Beast Hunter* as such. There's a famous quote regarding Occam's razor that goes something like, "When you hear hoof beats in the distance, you don't think it's a herd of unicorns. You think of horses, and you're probably correct." I also think of horses, but I'm willing to be shown the evidence for unicorns. I did have a "mistaken identity" theory for each cryptid in the series; however, I was more interested in the cultural significance of each myth than its veracity.

Early in the process of getting *Beast Hunter* green lit, Harry Marshall at Icon asked me to write a list of the 10 cryptids I was the most interested in researching in the field and why. I felt like Ralphie when he was asked to write a "Theme". Harry asked for ones where I felt there was a compelling and interesting story regardless of whether the animal was likely to be real or not. He wanted animals that *could* exist, not necessarily ones that I thought did. My first draft did not contain the Mongolian Death Worm, nor did my second draft, or third. These lists had animals like the Thylacine, a known but recently extinct marsupial wolf in Tasmania; the giant octopus, an alleged deep-sea cephalopod reaching sizes on a par with *Architeuthis dux*, the giant squid; Orang Pendek, the "little-bigfoot" of Sumatra; the Yeti, an alleged hominin from the Himalayas; Caddy, a sea serpent oft spotted off Canada's Vancouver Island, and others. Some made the cut eventually and their stories got told; most, sadly, did not. Harry's challenge to me with each draft was to think of this in terms of what story we could tell and what story people would want to see. What was interesting culturally about the thylacine? What could we say about the Yeti which hadn't already been told a thousand times? What could we actually film/who could we interview about the giant octopus? Was it in a misunderstood or under-featured region of the world? After four drafts we had the list for the Nat Geo executives:

1. Cobra Grande – Amazonia
2. The Thylacine / Megalania – New Zealand / Australia / Tasmania
3. The Mapinguari – Amazonia
4. Lake Labynkyr Monster – Siberia
5. Caddy – Vancouver

6. The Moa – New Zealand
7. Orang Pendek – Sumatra
8. Bili Ape – Democratic Republic of the Congo
9. Mokele M'bembe – West Africa
10. Giant Octopus / Lusca – The Caribbean

The night before our Nat Geo meeting, Harry, Laura Marshall (Co-founder and Managing Director), Andie (Director of Productions), and I were staying at the Tabard Inn in Washington DC. The Tabard is a fantastic hidden gem in a sea of nondescript DC chain hotels. Much like Harry himself, it is acutely eccentric without trying. And like Harry and Laura's lovely home in Bristol, there is something to discover in every corner of every room. If you've never been there, it's worth checking out the next time you're in DC. Harry looked over our list one last time while sipping a vodka rocks and said, slowly, "This is great, each story is compelling, hasn't been done to death on other networks, and will be visually incredible. I only have three issues with it. One, the locations – they're all jungles or bodies of water. Too much green and blue each week, people will get bored. Think of the trailers – nothing will stand out as a contrast, each episode will look the same, and the series teaser will look like it's for one long episode."

I hadn't thought of that at all, but he was absolutely right. "Two," he continued, "aside from this Russian lake, I've *seen* all of these places. They're all the most common hotspots for natural-history series. The Amazon? Indonesia? Australia? Laura, dear, I think we've filmed in all of these places in the last year, yes?"

"I'd have to go back to our logs to check, but in the last two definitely," Laura replied, setting down her wine.

"And last," continued Harry, "there isn't a name on this list that grabs you and draws you in. Nothing that, if you aren't already familiar with cryptozoology, makes you jump up and say, 'Yes! I want to know more about that!' You know? They're either common sounding or unpronounceable."

I smiled, "You're thinking about the Death Worm again, aren't you?" I said, as I tipped my scotch towards him in a salute.

Harry had been advocating for the Mongolian Death Worm since our first conversation and I'd been pushing back – I just couldn't see it. Everything about the Death Worm was outrageous. Admittedly, it is the most badass name for any animal; real or imaginary. It sounds like an eighties metal band or a creature Gozer the Gozerian would conjure and "sic" on NYC. And it only gets more outlandish when you describe its vast array of super powers. In fact, it's hard not to sound like a nine-year-old who has just read his first cryptozoology book and drank a Jolt Cola when describing it.

"And it can kill you with, like, lightning that it shoots like *pew-pew-pew* when it glows blue and gets all electric! And it shoots acid that melts through *bone!* It melts your *face* like, 'Ahhhhh! My face is covered in acid and melting!', and its blood is boiling hot and POISON! Did I say that already? Its blood is straight *poison!* Like, it kills you if it touches you, because the poison absorbs into your skin! Its skin is poison too! You can't touch one or you'll die! And it spits acid and poison blood at you! And sometimes, if it gets really mad, it EXPLODES! Phlew! Churrsshhhh! Explodes! Blaaaah! All over, and just sprays poison and blood and acid and lightning and everything!"

Yes, these are all supposed abilities of this creature. I saw the draw from a "holy crap, that sounds cool" perspective, but I couldn't see how this type of story fit our narrative.

"What do you *know* about this death worm?" Harry asked.

I shrugged. "Well, not much I guess. I basically wrote it off because it sounded too out there."

"*You* are supposed to be our 'open-minded skeptic', Pat, remember?" reprimanded Harry, smirking. "Let's talk through it a bit. I bet you know more than you think you do."

"Okay, fair point. Well, it's not supposed to be massive," I started. "Only a few feet long, I think."

"That doesn't sound outrageous," said a grinning Harry, looking over the top of his glasses. "I've heard not even a few feet – it's the size of a goat or sheep stomach, or something, yeah?"

"Yeah, I think you're right. Okay, so around a foot or two long, it's reddish in color, which I guess makes sense in a desert of sandstone." I was thinking out loud now. "It allegedly shoots hot blood or acid at people."

"Like a horned lizard," said Harry. "An animal you've worked with, I believe?"

"Yeah, okay, and like a bombardier beetle, which shoots hot acid," I added. "It also supposedly electrocutes people and blows itself up – like a blowfish and an electric eel." I saw Harry was about to say something. "Yeah, I see, I see – but an eel, an electric catfish, and an electric ray are all fish, and a lot of fish possess the ability to generate and release an electrical charge for navigation, prey location, etc. It makes sense that some would have evolved stronger pulses to incapacitate prey. We have no evidence that this trait ever evolved on land where a weak impulse would be virtually useless."

"Platypi," stated Harry, flatly. "I believe platypi use it to locate prey."

I searched my scotch-soaked memory. Yeah, he was right. "Okay, you've got me. But platypi are the *weirdest* animals, an aberration, and semi-aquatic. But, yeah, okay, we have a basis to see this in an at-least partially terrestrial animal."

"What else?" asked Harry, getting excited and taking another sip from his glass. "What do you know about Mongolia?"

I thought for a second. "Nothing, actually," I admitted.

"Exactly!" exclaimed a triumphant Harry. "Nothing! Because it really hasn't been done in natural-history programs. What do you know about the Gobi Desert? I can't think of very much. What do you know about Roy Chapman Andrews?"

"It's who Indiana Jones was based on?" I answered, unsure.

"Correct. How great a story is that? How amazing a location is that? Indiana Jones had multiple expeditions looking for this electrically charged, acid-spitting, burrowing creature in a region that was shut out of the world community for decades. That spawned Genghis Khan. The least populated country on Earth. A place where more fossils are found than anywhere else. A vast, unexplored, gorgeous desert that hardly anyone knows anything about. Think about it – think about the possibilities! What *could* be out there?"

Harry was right. I'd been doing what I accused so many other scientists of doing – writing something off without even hearing the facts. Neither Harry nor I thought we would find an animal meeting the description of the Death Worm, but he did convince me that there was a story worth telling in a land worth exploring, and a culture worth bringing into the spotlight. The Mongolian Death Worm went onto our list. "Sorry, Moa, you go to season two!" said an excited Harry as he scribbled on the pages of his ever-present notebook.

The moment the executives at Nat Geo read the words "Mongolian Death Worm" the next day, I knew I'd be traveling to the Gobi. The meeting was going well, everyone was polite, there were smiles all around, and then Laura passed around the list of potential episodes. Immediately, three people said, "Tell me more about this 'Mongolian Death Worm'! I love the way that sounds!"

Harry motioned for me to take over, and I did. I pitched everything we had discussed the night before. They were enthralled. We moved onto other animals, my background, etc., but it was the Death Worm that captured their interest, and, I believe, sold them on the series. The other potential episodes shifted until about two months before we left to film, but the

Death Worm was always on the list from that day forward.

Yes, after that meeting I knew we were heading to Mongolia. What I didn't know was how we were going to make this into an episode. The Death Worm was a bogeyman, I still thought, nothing more. Once again, I was wrong.

So, aside from the incomplete description above, what is the Mongolian Death Worm (MDW from here out)? It's generally described as an insect-like elongated creature with a segmented body whose head is indistinguishable from its tail. It is reddish, between one and three feet in length, and about six inches in diameter. It lives in the rocky, fertile regions of the Gobi Desert where it burrows underground, rarely surfacing, and its danger cannot be overstated.

Despite being approximately three times the size of France, Mongolia is only home to about 2.9 million people, or roughly the population of Paris, making it the most sparsely populated independent country in the world. More than half the population lives in Ulaanbaatar, the capital city. This leaves a lot of open space for a smallish, sand-colored, burrowing "worm" to go unnoticed. Sightings have stayed fairly consistent since the West heard of this creature in 1924, but peaked in the 1950s.

The Gobi is actually an extremely diverse ecosystem and can support all manner of life. It's not just sand dunes and barren landscapes, as you might imagine. I was shocked when I started researching it in earnest and saw swaths of trees, lots of desert plants, and rugged, rocky terrain in the images online. There were areas that looked suitable for grazing animals used by nomadic herders, whom we would live with, with others that looked like Tatooine, and everything in between.

Mongolia's interior was closed to outsiders throughout the Soviet era and has only recently been opened to explorers, which means there are almost certainly animals that have yet to be named – in fact, the largest species of lizard in Mongolia wasn't discovered until 1978. The more I researched the Death Worm, the more excited I became – not because I really believed we would find one, or one even existed, but because it was a story and a culture which few Westerners had experienced. Before we could head to Mongolia, though, we needed to write an episode around an animal that sounded as outlandish as anything out of *Harry Potter*.

While the traits associated with it seem fantastical (deadly to the touch, can electrocute you, spits acid/blood, blows itself up), all of these characteristics are found in known species, as Harry pointed out to me that night in DC. We wanted to show these superpowers in action using known animals, which meant I was going to be in nerd heaven once again. The picklist for animals was a dream come true. Did I want poison dart frogs, spitting cobras, electric eels, horned lizards, electric rays, bombardier beetles, pufferfish, or platypi? Yes, yes, and yes. I wanted them all. We started the process of figuring out which animals I could legally work with and in what countries. We were going to do a studio shoot – the only one of the series – in the US or England, as logistically these two countries made the most sense.

I recruited a friend, Gabe, who worked at a local zoo to see what he could get his hands on. He had access to poison dart frogs and horned lizards, but it turned out that transporting deadly animals across state lines is a little trickier than we anticipated. Gabe offered to buy some bombardier beetles and a spitting cobra from a legit reptile dealer, but was working on the details and legality of getting them to the filming location. Also, we'd then be responsible for figuring out what to do with these living creatures after filming. I'd been planning on borrowing an electric eel from another friend in New Hampshire, but the situation seemed to be spiraling into a place no one was entirely morally comfortable with. Gabe was very aware of all of the laws involved in this endeavor, and advised us that a few of the things we were planning could easily cross them. Just as I'd lined up another friend who would gladly take a free spitting cobra and a bunch of acid-expelling beetles (and who had the experience and facilities to actually care for these animals), Icon wisely decided to move the operation to England and work with people who owned these animals rather than acquiring them for ourselves. As cool as it would have been to have any of these creatures as an office mascot, they already had Alfie, Harry and Laura's parson terrier, so we found some Brits who would let us "rent" a couple of the species on our list for the day, and resolved to use stock footage for the rest.

We ended up with stock-footage of horned toads, scenes of a poison dart frog we'd shot in Costa Rica for *Nature Calls*, an electric eel rented from a private aquarist, and a spitting cobra provided by expert herpetologist and handler Mark Amey. Mark is amazing and is the man who supplied many of the creatures for the *Harry Potter* films, including the gorgeous reticulated python that played Nagini. A couple folks from Icon rigged up a rudimentary device made of two metal plates, wires, and a lightbulb. If sufficient electrical current hit the plates, the light bulb would glow. This was a great visual for the eel – which is not an eel at all but a rather dull-looking elongated knifefish native to the Amazon. Ours was about three feet – just long enough so that no doctor was confident in saying it *wouldn't* kill me if I received a full-power shock from it.

The original plan was to get a smallish one – preferably under the two-foot mark – and have me reach my hand in the tank and describe the sensation. This was my idea, like the bullet ants, and was fully vetted by health and safety. Everyone thought it actually sounded kind of fun, and a few crew members publicly stated they intended to join me. Some talk started about forming a human chain and causing lightbulbs to glow with our fingers, etc. All of this was dashed by the killjoy physicians, who said a firm "no" once they heard about the size of the only "rentable" eel in the country. The eel came with a tank, thick, shoulder-length, insulated gloves that made you look like Dr.

Frankenstein, and, disconcertingly, a long metal net – "just in case" – although this looked like the least likely fish to ever jump out of its tank.

The cobra was a Namibian Spitting Cobra and was a gorgeous dark olive green/brown. She was five feet long and Mark said her spray was accurate from about six feet. We had a high-speed camera and I was going to wear goggles and a face shield and entice the cobra to spit at my eyes. It all sounded straightforward and simple – half a day of shooting, five hours tops.

We arrived at an old British farmhouse outside Bristol at around 6am where we met Mark and found the electric eel at the bottom of its tank, not moving, in the exact same spot it had been when it was delivered the night before. I know reading that you're probably thinking it was dead – for a heart-racing moment we thought that too, but it wasn't, they just don't move very much. Lady Laura's journey in getting the eel deserves its own chapter, but I'll just say it was not an easy trip for woman or fish.

We went to work setting up lights, cameras, and mics. First up, the eel. I did a piece to camera about how it generates electricity, how powerful it is, and what could potentially happen to me if I were to grab it. As I was saying this I donned the thick gloves, more for cinematic effect than anything else. At the end of my speech I explained what the plates were for and started to insert them in the water. The first plate went in and the eel didn't even wiggle. I explained how poor its eyesight was owing to the fact that it normally lives in muddy, murky pools in the Amazon, and their hunting and defense strategy was basically, "shock first, ask questions later". I postulated how many volts it was giving off in "exploratory shocks". I used to volunteer at the New England Aquarium and was fascinated by the huge electric eel they had there. I was able to talk to the main aquarist who cared for her and bombarded her with questions every time we spoke, so I felt pretty confident in what

I was saying. I started to put the second plate in, and as soon as it touched the water the lethargic fish freaked the F out. The thing bolted towards the plate, and when it touched it leapt out of the water. I instinctively pulled the plate out and blocked the fish with my hand, thanking God I had the gloves on.

The fish felt like solid muscle, I could feel its strength even with the thick rubber glove. It sank back into the tank as the crew yelled "cut" and tried to figure out what had just happened. We decided to try again, but this time we were ready with the net and another gloved person from Icon to help. Once again, when the plate touched the water, the fish decided it wanted out. We blocked it again, then decided the shot was not worth the stress it was causing to the poor thing. We never figured out what was happening. I've asked aquarists and they have no idea. Some postulated that it sensed the circuit the two plates created and thought it was a bigger eel in the water, but none really know. Maybe we just lucked out and happened to receive a psychotic fish. We filmed a couple minutes of me looking at the eel through the tank and decided these would be the only shots we'd get with it. We covered the tank and let it go back to doing what electric eels do best – resting on the bottom and not really moving.

The cobra was next. Before taking it out of its excessively marked cooler – brightly colored danger stickers everywhere proclaiming a deadly creature was contained within, listing various numbers to call should this crate be opened, and assuring the opener that they would die should they proceed with undoing the latches – Mark made a speech to us about just how dangerous the snake was. "Right, so what we have here is a Namibian Spitting Cobra. She's a good girl and I've worked with her a lot. You've probably seen her spit on a few nature show hosts before, in fact, but that doesn't mean she's a puppy. She's docile, but can and will bite if I do something wrong. She can strike almost the length of her body, and spit even further, so I want everyone but Pat to be at least 10 feet away from her at all times, preferably further. That means if she moves, you move. I will have control of her the whole time, but if I lose that control don't panic. She'll likely just try to take cover somewhere. Let her. Do not, I repeat, do not try to grab her for any reason. I'm the only one who should touch her – well, and maybe Pat. Are you okay with that if you need to?"

A little terrified, I nodded. "Yeah."

"You've handled these before?"

"Never a spitter, but I've worked with cobras. Spectacled and kings."

"Okay, great. Very similar, and you'll have the face shield, so don't worry about the spitting." He went back to addressing everyone. "We all know about the spitting, and that's not fun, but it won't kill you and will only blind you if you don't wash the venom out. I have an eyewash kit should anyone get hit in the eyes. That's not the venom that worries me though, as she can, and will, bite. Her venom is a mix of cytotoxins, neurotoxins, and cardiotoxins. What that means is it will hurt like hell, melt your flesh, and make it hard to breathe. In fact, the way you'd die is asphyxiation should it come to that, which it won't. These snakes have a nasty venom, but, relatively speaking, it's not *that* nasty. It will mess you up, you may lose the limb you are bitten on, but you will likely not die. If I get bitten though, it will be bad. I've been bitten before and had a nasty reaction. This is very important." He held up a card. "This is the number *you* call if *I* get bitten. The people here will know what to do and what antivenin I need. Got it?" We all nodded. "Okay, good. Now, let's have some fun. Let's see the setup before I bring this beautiful girl out to play."

Laura showed Mark the black tablecloth-covered surface where the cobra would be filmed. A very expensive high-speed camera was set up next to it to capture incredible slo-mo images. We had tested the shot using a rubber cobra, which was still sitting placidly on the surface, very well lit. Mark laughed and grabbed it, pretending to struggle. The plan was to have the snake on the approximately eight-foot-long table with Mark holding her tail off camera and me at the other end, about four feet away with my face shield on. Mark would position her so she could rear up to about my height if I leaned down a bit, and spit straight into my face. Sounded easy on paper and Mark said he'd done this shot a dozen times and it shouldn't be a problem. After the electric-eel debacle we hoped he was right. Just to make sure, we mimicked the whole thing using our "stunt cobra", and it looked beautiful.

I was given nitrile gloves, because "the venom burns if it gets on your skin", but my forearms were bare as my dress shirt was rolled up almost to the elbow. Mark ran through another safety check, made sure everyone was clear from the strike zone, and opened the cooler. There was an audible gasp from everyone as the snake poured out and onto the table, hood opened fully. There is such a primal reaction that humans have to snakes. It's universal. They elicit awe – not necessarily fear, but always awe. If you've never seen a cobra in person without glass separating you from it, trust me, it's different to any other snake.

The first thing you notice, of course, is the hood. It's something you've seen in a million books and movies, but seeing it in person is a different thing all together. You see it go from a wormlike reptile to an ageless symbol of death in a millisecond. Next you notice their eyes, which seem larger and more intelligent than most snakes. They have a large, round pupil as opposed to the beady cat eyes of most venomous snakes Americans are used to. There seems to be a calm behind those eyes that is startling, a restraint. Rattlesnakes always seem angry to me – some, like Mojaves, are almost manic, unhinged. Cobras on the other hand always seem to be thinking, like they are deciding if they're going to shake your hand or shoot you, and like a gunslinger they're waiting for you to make the first move, knowing they're quicker.

The first cobra I held was in captivity and I didn't know what it was right away. A woman handed me a five-foot snake and I draped it around my neck, as you do with captive, docile, large snakes, and took a look. She asked if I knew what kind of snake it was. It was an olive green with large scales and large eyes. The snake's tail started digging into my arm, like it was trying to puncture me. "That's odd," I thought. "That's a cobra thing, isn't it? She couldn't have just handed me a cobra though, right?" Realization slowly dawned on me when I moved its head closer to mine to get a good look at the face and head scales. Yup, this looked like a green cobra. But cobras aren't green, right? With the snake's large head staring right at me from about a foot away, I said, hesitantly, "Is this a cobra?"

"Yeah, a king! You got it!" and she pulled on the snake's body a little to get it to hood – again, about a foot away from my face. "Most people get really thrown by the color."

Holy shit, I was holding a king cobra. "Is it venomoid?" I asked, trying not to show my fear. Venomoid snakes are very controversial and still considered dangerous – the animal has usually had an operation to remove or somehow inhibit the venom glands, but the snake can "heal" and reverse the procedure unbeknownst to the handler, or could suffer and even die due to the surgery.

"Nope, he's fully hot. But really friendly, don't worry about it."

I calmly, but quickly, handed the snake back to this person. I don't care how "calm" your venomous snake is, I'm not going to free-handle it.

Mark, being much more reasonable, kept a hold of the snake's tail and allowed it to get used to the new situation it found itself in before asking it to "perform". He explained that the snake was taking the scene in and we should be patient and not expect anything. At which point, the snake spat. Just a quick burst, right into my eyes – at least it would have been, if I hadn't been wearing the face shield. The accuracy was shocking. I hadn't even known it was looking at me, and here was a direct hit from more than five feet away. "Woah" was all any of us could muster.

Mark just smiled. "She's a good girl, I told you. Okay, well, looks like she's ready, let's see if I can get her up, yeah? Cameras good?" Cameras were rolling, and Lorne from Icon gave the thumbs up. "Okay, here we go. Pat, lean in like we talked about," said Mark, and moved her tail a little as I leaned in so I was maybe three feet from her. She reared up, but only about six inches, not the more than a foot we were expecting, and, without hooding, spat again – a full, solid shot right into my face. "Spitting" isn't exactly accurate. They bare their fangs and a stream of liquid shoots from the front of them, pumped by unseen muscles in their necks and body. It's more like a squirt gun than an animal spitting at you. This shot, like the last one, hit me right in the eyes.

Our segment producer, who was watching the whole thing from his monitor, said the lighting was off and there were strange shadows. He asked to add some bright lights and try it again. Lorne and a couple others scrambled to turn on the lights while I kept the snake's full attention by moving my hands in a jerky "look at me" manner. I was hit in the face a few more times for my trouble. The venom is like saliva – the snake produces it constantly and doesn't "run out", but they do get tired of spitting after a while, when it's not having the intended effect, namely incapacitating me, or at least making me run away. To prevent this from happening, Mark asked me to keep her attention with slow, loping movements, like a snake charmer. I did this and was impressed to watch her head follow me in miniscule, slow movements mimicking mine.

The lights were set, Lorne gave the thumbs up, the cameras rolled, and I leaned in for another hit. This one went high, into my hair. The next five or six shots hit my chest, my chin, my arms, and everywhere except my eyes. She also hadn't once reared up to her full height. We took another break and Lorne repositioned the lights after Mark said they were throwing off her aim. While that was going on, and as I was keeping the snake's attention, I asked Mark why she wasn't raising and hooding.

"Yeah, I've been thinking about that too. I think it's twofold – she doesn't feel threatened, so good for you for staying calm, mate!"

"I'm not a very intimidating guy," I agreed.

"And two, I don't think she can get a solid grip on this cheap tablecloth." He reached out to feel it. "See, have a feel."

I did, and he was right. It was a blended fabric that had almost a slick to it. It looked really nice on camera, but for a snake used to sand, gravel, and forest floor it wasn't providing the traction she needed to feel confident in holding her head up too high.

"What should we do?" I asked Mark.

"Not much to do at this point. The shot is almost always in the first five minutes. After that, she gets too comfortable. I think we've already missed our window. Let's break and retry after lunch, yeah?"

We announced our plans to the producer, who looked a little worried. We'd failed on the eel, now the snake wasn't looking much better, but with no options he agreed. Mark moved the snake back into her container and I took my face mask off. I was shocked to find how much venom was on it, and on me. Most of it had dried into little crystals on my shirt and arms and looked like glistening salt. I also hadn't realized how much of my attention had been focused on the snake until she was safely in her container. As my focus was no longer diverted I noticed that my arms and head were burning. I told Mark and he started laughing, telling me to go scrub my arms and head in the sink.

"And keep your eyes closed!" he added as I walked away. "If your eyes start burning tell me right away!"

I did as he advised and came back feeling a lot better, but exhausted. I think being on high alert that entire time had drained all my energy. We left the room and had some lunch and coffee. We shared travel stories for about 20 minutes before a nervous-looking producer suggested we get back to it. Unfortunately, the next two hours went much as the first fifteen minutes had. Despite making adjustments to the surface the snake was on, we couldn't get the lighting right without affecting its aim and freaking it out, causing it to retreat from the bright lights. We also couldn't get a surface that the snake could cling to and allow it to rear up and fully hood. We did get dozens of shots of it spitting from a slightly raised position. I must have gotten hit with venom 30 times that day. By the end of the two hours, the distance between me and the cobra had shrunk to about two feet as she required increasingly threatening movements to get her to strike. Counterintuitively, because of the dual protection the mask provided, I had to lead with my face and keep my hands way back. It was bizarre to see a cobra strike at you and not put your hands up to block it. Towards the end, I noticed my eyes starting to water, then saw the same was happening to Mark, who was also coughing a little.

"How long have we been at this?" Mark said after a little cough.

"About two hours, give or take," replied Lorne.

Mark looked my way, saw my eyes watering, motioned at them and said, "When did that start?"

"Just a second ago, actually. You too?" I asked.

"Yup." Mark thought a second, then said, "Okay, folks, we are wrapping this up and we're clearing out. Open the windows and doors as soon as she's put away." He motioned to the snake. "Pat and I are going to get some air." Using a snake stick, Mark expertly placed the cobra back in her bin and unceremoniously closed and checked all of the latches. "Walk with me, Pat," he said.

We walked outside, then into a new room with a large sink. "Wash your hands, arms, head, and face." I did as instructed, and then Mark did the same. "Two hours, bloody hell, the time just got away from me." He mused, "She must've spit, what, 20, 30 times?" I guessed about that. "Mate, we've breathed in enough venom that it's starting to burn our mucus membranes."

That did not sound good. "Is that bad?" I asked, stupidly. "Do we need to go to the hospital?"

"Well, it's not good, but it's not terrible," replied a very calm Mark. "I wouldn't take up smoking this week, eh?" He laughed and coughed. "Honestly, it's not a problem, just an irritant really. I've breathed it in before, just never this much, I reckon. No worries, though, we'll both be fine. Everyone else was probably far enough away where they won't feel a thing."

I felt a little better, but was still concerned. "Is there anything I should do? Signs I should watch out for?"

"I'd take a long shower tonight, a real good soak. Keep your eyes closed while you wash your hair. You'll be fine, mate, don't worry." He must have seen the look of concern on my face. "This is a good one to tell people about later! Not many people, even hardcore reptile people, can say they've breathed in venom like we did today!"

And so the least productive and most dangerous shoot in *Beast Hunter* ended.

Once we were in Mongolia, memories of the eel and snake shoot already seemed distant. So did any thoughts that this shoot was a bad idea, or that the Death Worm was an absurd story to pursue. I have never been in a place where an electricity-producing worm seemed more like a possibility. Everything about the Gobi is alien, nothing about it makes sense. You can drive for a day without seeing any sign of humans, and then come across a ger, and unexpectedly bump into a person you met a week before in Ulaanbaatar. "Oh, you live here! Nice to see you again. Yes, I'd love some fermented mare's milk, thank you." So. Weird. Add in the nest of dinosaur eggs I found while walking around and how do you even wrap your head around a place where you find dinosaur eggs on the ground in 2010?

So, the million dollar question after that long intro – do I think that there is a smallish wormlike animal that shoots electricity, hot acid, boiling blood, and poison, occasionally blows itself up, and is toxic to the touch? No, I do not. Yes, these things all exist in nature in other animals, but I saw absolutely no evidence that an animal like that lives in the Gobi Desert. I also saw an ecosystem that would not drive any of those traits to evolve, and probably wouldn't provide enough energy to sustain those superpowers, unless it somehow became solar-powered and was okay with hibernating below the frostline during the brutal winters Mongolia was subject to. I just can't see it.

Then what, you might ask, do I think is behind the stories? Are the Mongolian nomadic herders liars? Are these tall tales to scare their kids into not straying far from the ger? Is this a bogeyman? A living manifestation of the harshness of the desert? Are the stories meant to be symbolic, a representation of the horrors the desert can exert on a person? These are all questions I can, and will, answer.

Are the Mongolian nomads liars?

No, not in my experience. Unlike some of the people I encountered while filming this show, not a single herder in Mongolia seemed disingenuous. No one seemed to be telling these stories for fame, mostly because "fame" was meaningless to them. There was no TV in anyone's ger, and they didn't care that people they didn't know might hear or see them. There was no money involved in them telling their stories. We didn't bring excessive gifts, and this certainly wasn't going to draw tourists.

The nomads we encountered were some of the kindest,

gentlest, and most honest people I have ever come across. They told us what they knew, and admitted what they didn't know. They welcomed us into their homes, shared what they had, and asked for nothing in return. I have no reason to suspect them of lying or exaggerating any tales of the death worm, because they didn't lie or exaggerate any other stories they told.

Are stories of the death worm tall tales to scare their kids into not straying far from the ger?

Yes, I think so, but not in the same way as a boogeyman, where adults know they are tricking their kids. The nomads live a very, very hard life. Just breathing was difficult for us in the incredibly dry, sandy, baking heat. We all had sore throats by the 5th day. They live in either the brutal, oven-like heat of up to 130 degrees in summer, or some of the coldest temperatures on the populated Earth at -60 degrees in winter. The temperature can fluctuate by as much as 65 degrees in a single day. They are miles, possibly days or weeks, away from any medical attention. It is in their best interest to not take risks or get hurt. This doesn't play well in a teenage boy's psyche.

Kids, boys in particular, do really stupid things regularly. I'm speaking from experience. Parents must try to minimize the chance of death while encouraging a modicum of independence. Mongolian children are known as the most independent kids in the world. The nomad children might be herding a flock of goats on their own before many kids in the US are able to recite their alphabet. It is not generally advisable to investigate something new in these conditions. I didn't find that imaginative games were encouraged. It's best to assume that everything you encounter is dangerous, and if it's not an immediate threat just leave it be. This also plays into the deep-rooted Buddhism of the region.

"Live and let live" is not just an intellectual concept in Mongolia, it's ingrained in their very being. Where a kid in the

US would see a leaf on a tree as they walk by and pick it just to have something to do with their hands, a boy the same age in the Gobi couldn't imagine doing such a thing. In the US, you will see adults who still hit the top of a doorframe with their hands as they walk through it. I challenge you to find a nomad who does the same. Everything I observed was that nomads *observe*, but don't touch or explore. They watch, but rarely interact. They can stay stock still for hours, while we Westerners would start fidgeting in seconds. It was startling to have a conversation with a family of nomads who all sat quietly, making eye contact but not moving their bodies at all. No one playing with a phone, or picking their nails, or scratching their faces, even. They smile, laugh, speak kindly (please don't get the impression they were at all robotic), but are not fidgeters, and not the type to see a strange animal in the desert and decide to get a closer look.

It's little wonder that most of the stories associated with the death worm involve someone messing with it – someone poked it with a stick, then it killed them; someone dumped gasoline on it, then it killed them; a camel stepped on one, then it killed them, etc. No stories go "someone took a nap in the desert, and when they woke up a death worm was attacking them," or "someone got lost in the desert, and when they were trying to figure out what to do a death worm ambushed them." No – each story implies that if the now-dead person had just left the thing be, they would not be dead.

I don't think this was a purposeful "life lesson" from parents, I think it's just ingrained in them. I believe it's just something that makes sense to them. You mess with something you don't know and it can kill you, therefore you don't mess with something you don't know. It's unimaginable to think that a 10-year-old American boy would come across a two-foot-long wormlike creature and *not* poke it with a stick, and it's equally unimaginable that you'd come across a 10-year-old Mongolian nomadic boy who *would*. We just approach things from such a different place.

With that in mind, I don't think parents consciously know it's a tall tale, they just have no desire to prove or disprove it because it doesn't affect them. Of all the creatures I investigated, the Mongolian Death Worm's existence generated the least amount of excitement among the native populations where it was seen. I would ask, "Have you ever heard of the Mongolian Death Worm?" and they would answer, "Yes, I've heard of a nomad who was killed by one," or something similar. "I'm here to investigate the stories like that and see what I can find." The response to that was overwhelmingly puzzlement: "Why? Why would you want to investigate that?" I asked a couple people, "Wouldn't you like to know more about it?" and the response was a bland, "Sure?" Like, "I'm good either way." It really wouldn't affect their lives if we found it. Asking them about the death worm felt like if your doctor told you that you had a previously undetectable virus, but you've had it your whole life, and it could kill you, but there is a 99.999% chance that it won't ever affect you at all, then told you everyone on Earth had the virus, then asked you if you believed them. You'd probably be really worried for a few minutes, until you thought about it and realized everyone has it, and you've always had it, then you'd think it was weird if they asked you if you believed them. "Yeah – you're a doctor, I believe you." But, when the doctor asked for the 5th or 6th time if you believed them, you'd start to think it was really weird, and probably look for a new doctor. You also probably wouldn't be too concerned about it once you found out there was nothing you could do about this worldwide pandemic.

If the death worm was out there and they saw one, they would leave it alone and it wouldn't do anything to them, but they knew it was really unlikely they'd ever see one. If it wasn't out there, same outcome. They weren't going to go looking for it, and if they happened to find one they weren't going to poke it with a stick. Its existence or lack of existence had no real impact on their lives, and unlike everyone on Facebook they weren't going to get all worked up about something that had no real impact on their lives. They didn't feel the need to tell anyone that the other person's opinion was wrong, but it was one of the many things they warned their kids about. It wasn't so much, "don't go poking a death worm if you find one," more "don't touch anything because everything can kill you." There's an important distinction between the two.

Are the stories meant to be symbolic? A living manifestation of the harshness of the desert? A representation of the horrors the environment can exert on a person?

Like above – sort of, yes, but mostly no. I believe that when the nomads think about the death worm, they think about a real animal, not a story. But, at the same time, Buddhism does attach symbolism to real animals, places, and all living things. They even have cryptids as symbolic representations – the dragon, snow lion, and birdlike Garuda are important representations of various desirable traits. There is also a rich storytelling tradition in Mongolia. The Mongolian nomadic herders are spread across great distances and news used to be transmitted primarily by riders traveling on horseback from one location to another. Much of their history as a people has been captured in song and passed down in an oral tradition. There were famous bards, poets, and storytellers who would travel from ger to ger, welcomed by the world-famous Mongolian hospitality which I experienced firsthand, in exchange for their songs. Many of the songs and stories are deeply symbolic and allegorical, with some of the best bards themselves inspiring epics to be sung about them long after they passed away.

To this day, many of the most popular songs among the nomads are about horses – the symbol of the beauty, freedom, and wildness of the Gobi. Is it a stretch to think that stories of the death worm sprang from a need to symbolically represent the flipside of such a harsh environment? It can burn you, like the sun; it corrodes metal, like the environment of the desert itself; it doesn't bother those who treat it with respect, and it burrows through the soil – the nomads are not farmers, and the plants the Gobi supports must have seemed mystical to ancient herders who were so dependent on them for their flock, but had nothing to do with planting or tending to them. I believe there is a case to be made for saying horses represent all that is good in the Gobi, and the Death Worm all that is bad. There are even stories claiming that the thundering gallop of a horse can drive away the death worm – symbolically, good conquering evil.

Yes, the stories of the death worm are full of symbolism – but they aren't full of mythical monsters. The nomads believe that at the heart of the stories is a real creature, just as the horses symbolize good but are real animals – the death worm may embody the dangers of the Gobi, but it's just as real to them as their horses.

So where do the stories come from?

Like all recent terrible horror movies, I believe they are "based on a true story". As stated above, the nomads have a rich and allegorical storytelling tradition. They also tend to shy away from the unknown, not having that deeply ingrained American sense of entitlement towards the natural world. On top of this, they have a propensity for unknowingly – because they don't particularly care to prove these tales wrong – exaggerating the traits of known animals, and to an extreme extent.

I've described my crushing defeat at Bakh – traditional Mongolian Wrestling, and the most beloved of the "three manly skills" of the Naadam festival – in detail, and despite this emasculating rout I was able to regain all of the respect I lost and leave many nomads venerating me as the bravest, baddest guy they'd met by simply catching a bunch of harmless animals. They also thought I was a bit touched in the head, but in an incredibly daring way. The nomads, as a general rule, do not seek out new animals.

They have amazing stories and legends about known animals – those regarding falcons, snow leopards, and horses are well documented. Lesser known in the tomes written about these remarkable people are the traits and stories they associate with nearly every living thing they encounter. On our first day in the Gobi I had the good fortune of having an afternoon to explore while the crew filmed a reenactment – aptly, it was the story of a young boy poking a death worm with a stick and receiving his just rewards. After helping carry the gear and set up the shot, I was free for a couple glorious hours of catching anything I could find. As I did not have to look cool for a camera, I donned my preferred desert gear of a floppy green explorer hat, glasses rather than contacts, a snake stick, a butterfly net, and a couple reptile bags and pillowcases strung around my belt. As I geared up I felt the same way I did when doing this since being five years old – the unbridled joy of the unknown that was to greet me as soon as I stepped out of sight of the nearest adult. I had no idea what I'd find, if anything, but the search was at least 70% of the fun. It always has been. Some people go birding, I go herping. I will never understand why it's any weirder to travel and hike to find snakes than it is to travel and hike to find birds, and yet saying, "I'm a birder," at a day job gets you sucked into a polite, inquisitive conversation, whereas saying, "I'm a herper," gets you confused looks like you've just announced you have the heebie-jeebies, or, once you explain what herping is, disgust. Birds and reptiles are closely related and just as diverse in form, color, behavior, and environment. Why can't birders and herpers get the same treatment?

Well, I was off herping, like hundreds of times before – but this was the Gobi Desert! I saw agamids and geckos scurry away into thorny shrubs, I gave chase to a couple racerunners and watched with childlike joy as they dove into burrows, away from my halfhearted attempts to snatch them up. I grabbed a couple beetles of unknown lineage and studied them as they crawled on my arms, and then, as I swept a heavy-booted foot over some low-lying scrub brush to scare out whatever was hiding within, that squiggle of movement which can only be made by a frightened snake caught my eye and narrowed my focus.

When I spot a snake a lot happens in a millisecond. My initial instinct is to grab it – and has been since I was in diapers, according to my family. There is something so foreign, so "other", about a snake that, in my mind, it's impossible to not want to know more. Everything about them is "wrong" – how they move, their eyes, the way they curl up or shoot forward in a seemingly unpredictable and impossibly fast motion, their striking distance, their ability to inflict pain so fast you may not even notice you've been bitten until the adrenaline wears off (as has happened with me countless times), and that primal revulsion that all people seem to feel. Even those of us that love snakes and have channeled it into more a respect than a fear see that it's impossible to not be fascinated by these animals that inspire such a visceral response. There are so many kinds of snakes – from the gorgeous, almost feathered-looking rough-scaled bush viper (*Atheris hispida*) to the Massachusetts state reptile, the common garter snake (garter – not garden – named for their stripes, which appeared similar to men's garters to the early colonists) – but all inspire that "fight or flight" reflex. How can you not be fascinated by a harmless animal that can make 300 pound football players run and scream like frightened children at the mere sight of them? What is it that has been so ingrained in us evolutionarily that an entire suborder of animals is so reviled?

I see a snake, I fight the urge to immediately catch it, and start cycling through my mind, searching for an answer to one question: "Can this kill me?" If the answer is "no", I grab it. If the answer is "yes" or "I'm not sure", I try to stop it from getting away until I figure out a logical next move. In order to ascertain this, I don't have to know the species necessarily, I can look at its head, eyes, and markings and make an educated guess. A lot of those initial guesses fall into the "maybe" category. Luckily for me, the slender grey snake I spotted in Mongolia was an immediate "no". There are only a few species of venomous snake in Mongolia, and this was clearly not one of them. I grabbed it and it struck at me, over and over, hitting my hand but never actually biting. It moved so fast! The strike was shockingly quick – 2-3 hits in a second! Wild. Such a feisty little guy. I tossed him into one of the pillowcases I had brought and started walking back to the crew.

When I proudly showed them the fruits of my labor, the nomads we were with literally jumped backwards and yelled in horror. "Don't touch that! What are you doing? You are *crazy!*"

"It's just a racer, guys, he's not dangerous at all."

"Not dangerous? Are you crazy? He will kill you!"

I started to doubt myself – had I mis-ID'd this snake? Was it an unknown species of viper? No, it was definitely a colubrid, I was sure of it. I grabbed some pages I'd printed of common species in Mongolia which were serving as a field guide and identified it as a steppe ribbon racer – a fairly common species in Mongolia. I tried to pronounce its Mongolian name and the guides agreed, yes, same snake.

"How can this kill me?" I asked. "Its head is so small I don't think it could even bite me if it wanted to, which it does. Look, it keeps trying to bite, and can't." I showed them how it kept striking at me, but couldn't get a bite. Finally, the little guy did draw some blood, but it could just as easily have been a cut from the thorny plants I'd been playing in for the last hour that I just didn't notice before. I really wasn't sure.

The biggest of the nomads who was with us told me, through a translator, that it's not just the bite to worry about. In fact, the real danger is their tail. He told me, "These snakes are very fast. You see how fast they strike." I agreed. What he said next really shocked me, though. "These snakes, they curl in the sand, near some underbrush, and when you ride by on your camel, they shoot out, like a spring, and shoot through your camel, sticking into you and killing you! They miss a lot and just injure the camel's legs, though."

This sounded ridiculous at first, and I tried to explain how this was physiologically impossible. Many snakes around the world earn a reputation for "jumping" because they strike so fast. There are a couple species that truly do strike almost their entire body length, but "jumping" is a huge exaggeration, and leaping off the ground, through a camel, and into a person is something that I'm not even sure a bullet could do, much less a snake. I tried to explain that the snake would have to be made of steel, and their muscles would have to be able to generate a bullet-like force to accomplish this, but they wouldn't hear it. These animals were deadly. End of story.

I started to think about it. Clearly, no one who had this fate befall them lived to tell about it, so the stories would have spread after finding a body. These snakes primarily eat insects and small lizards, both of which would gather around a decomposing body of a man or a camel. A body would also not go unmolested by the scavengers of the desert – birds, foxes, etc. At first glance, it would be hard to tell what wounds caused the death and what occurred postmortem. Many scavengers are known to start their process of eating a corpse – and there's no polite way to say this – butt first. Many animals, including humans, are known to empty their bowels close to the time of death, and the intestines contain nutrients that are hard to come by, such as partially digested plant matter that is vitamin-rich for a carnivorous scavenger. Plus, it's an "easy access" point into the body cavity where all of the good bits are. Animals want to eat the rich organs first, but the hide of many animals is hard to get through. So, you walk up to the bodies of a camel and a person, and there are multiple deep wounds on both, including a hole into the person's butt, which was presumably sitting on the camel. You see a snake which is known to strike incredibly fast slithering away as you approach, or worse, also striking at you. Thinking about this, it suddenly doesn't seem like such a stretch to assume that the snake killed the camel and impaled the poor violated nomad.

The other comment about them "missing a lot" was also telling. Like I said, this snake was fast and aggressive, if ineffectual in its strikes. It's also called an "arrow snake" because of its pointed head and tail and the quick, straight strikes it makes. Imagine riding your camel through the desert and occasionally seeing a snake striking at its lumbering feet. When you get off your steed you notice bloody wounds covering its legs. Logic tells you they are probably from the thorny underbrush you've been walking through, but what if it was the snake? Best to be safe and assume it was the snake.

By catching and actually holding this snake, I was immediately elevated in the nomads' eyes. I was beyond brave. These hulking, chiseled, tough guys wanted to take pictures with me while I held the snake, far away from them. The bravest would stand next to me and touch my arm with one finger while I held the snake facing away from them. That's as close as they were willing to get. I couldn't persuade any of them to even touch it. Amazingly, and unlike many Americans, although they were terrified of it, when it came time to let it go no one suggested I kill it. They believed that this harbinger of death had as much a right to live as they did, and asked that I return it to as close to where I found it as possible. (Have I mentioned that I love the nomads in Mongolia? Because I love the nomads in Mongolia.)

It wasn't just snakes that terrified them. I caught a cute little toad-faced agama – a tiny lizard that looks a lot like a regal horned lizard – and again was scolded for picking this up. "They are so dangerous! I can't believe you are holding that! Actually, you will probably be okay."

"Why, what's dangerous about this little guy?" I asked, as I let him climb around on my face.

"They eat babies."

Toad-faced agamas do eat babies – baby crickets, but definitely not baby humans. I tried not to think too deeply about how this legend started as it's just too sad to think about the reality of an infant mortality rate in such harsh conditions. I'm sure a lot of animals have an unfortunate reputation for "eating babies", especially ones that actually eat insects which are attracted to recently dead bodies.

One night we were out filming using night-vision goggles and I came across a mole cricket, a largish, very bizarre insect that spends the vast majority of its life underground. It has huge front legs shaped like a mole's digging claws, a long slender body, tiny little wings, and various spiky appendages. "Mole cricket" is the perfect common name actually, because it really looks like a mole and a cricket somehow had a very ugly baby. The nomads with us were already on edge – they did not like exploring the desert at night, and did not like digging in the dirt. When this weird creature came to the surface it seemed to validate all of their fears.

"Oh no, don't touch that!" they yelled when I moved like I was going to catch it.

"Why? What is it?" I asked, just to see what they would say.

They paused and spoke to each other in Mongolian for about 30 seconds before one answered. "We don't know. No one has ever seen one, but it looks very dangerous. It looks like the front legs could tear into you, and the head could burrow through your skin. Those spines on its legs and back look like thorns, and we think they contain venom and poison. You should not touch it, or I think you will die. Just leave it, walk away, and it will go back into the ground."

I picked it up and explained what it was, telling them how they burrow through the ground looking for roots, grubs, worms, and smaller insects. I explained they can bite, but aren't dangerous at all. They are not poisonous or electric (knowing that they can vibrate their wings and their hard exoskeleton, and rub their legs and body together, all of which can sometimes feel like a hand buzzer when you hold one). Because they had no preconceived notions about this animal, having never seen one, they were brave and agreed to touch it, but acted like teenagers, daring each other and laughing nervously after barely brushing it with one finger. The cricket emitted a bad-smelling, dark liquid, and they immediately thought this was blood or poison, or both. I explained it was just a defense mechanism. I also explained about stridulation – the "singing" of the mole cricket (rubbing their legs on their body to produce sound) – which it does to attract a mate, but which we can sense as a small vibration if we're near their burrow. They dig holes and "call" inside them, which can be loud enough to shake the ground.

Hearing them make up traits for this animal on the spot really got me thinking about the "superpowers" of the death worm. I decided to dig around a little more – figuratively and literally. I found some grubs in the dirt – again, they had never seen them, but didn't want to touch them. I found a few other little burrowing insects, all of which were unknown. I was shocked. These were not rare insects, they were bountiful, found in the first four shovel loads of Earth I ever scooped in the Gobi. Yet the nomads had lived there all of their lives and never seen them. And then I had my theory for the truth behind the death worm.

Like many others before me, I've come to believe that the death worm is a misidentification of several known and possibly a couple unknown species. I believe this for many reasons, all observed firsthand:

- The nomads do not, as a general rule, seek out unknown animals, and really don't recognize many common species that are either nocturnal or fossorial.
- Nomad children are taught to observe, but not interfere with, most wildlife as part of their deep-seated respect for all life.
- They ascribe extraordinary superpowers to harmless, known animals.
- Wildlife legends are important to the culture of the area.
- The Gobi supports a vast diversity of life – much more than many Western readers would think – and is unexplored enough where there are likely a few new species in its vast expanse.
- Stories travel fast (remember my wrestling re-enactment experience?) and details tend to get blurred.

A bit more speculation is in order, I think, so here are some potential death worm candidates.

Snakes

This is the most obvious candidate, particularly a venomous species or sand boa. Does it check the boxes, though?

- Color? Check.
- Size? Check.
- Shape? Check.
- "Head and tail look the same"? Check.
- Burrowing? Check.
- Electric? – no. But:
  - It would "crackle" like electricity if a camel stepped on it.

- Snakes do "shake" sometimes, seeming to vibrate with electric energy – I know that's a stretch, but it doesn't take much to spark a great story. They do this when sick, caring for their eggs (shaking generates body heat to warm the eggs), and for other reasons.
- The expression "striking fast as lightning" is not limited to the English language.

- Exploding? Maybe, but note that the explanations rely less on the death worm being a snake and more on a snake simply being present near the scene, and therefore apply to all the candidates below:
  - A decaying corpse in the hot sun can fill with gas and can "explode" due to a buildup of gas from bacteria typically present in the gut. This is more common with larger animals (cows and whales – less "explosion" and more "gas-buildup and release"), but it isn't unreasonable to think that people had found bloated, decaying camel or even human corpses that looked like something had exploded in or near it.
  - A bloated animal that a camel or person stepped on would explode, sometimes with an audible noise. I have seen this phenomena more than once and it can be very surprising when you're not expecting it, and also hard to explain if you don't know the science of decomposition.
  - The liquids that come out of such a rotting corpse are often hot to the touch, and the smell is revolting, both traits can make these liquids seem more dangerous than they are.
  - Predation by certain animals – particularly birds – can cause an animal to appear to have "exploded" when they only remove certain organs like the heart or stomach.
  - A bigger stretch, but still entirely possible, could be

natural gas pockets. The Gobi is rich in natural gas and these deposits are known to be volatile. It isn't unreasonable to think that, in the long history of the Gobi, a couple have gone off on their own or aided by a discarded cigarette, and caused some havoc. Such explosions would have dislodged chunks of Earth, uncovering and killing the animals within – animals like sand boas.

- Touching it can cause death? Maybe, in my experience, some snakes can bite you without you realizing it right away, especially when your adrenaline is way up from having come across a snake unexpectedly. It's possible that a nomad didn't realize they'd been bitten, then died from the bite thinking it was just from touching the animal. This would be more believable for a neurotoxic snake, however – where the venom kills you by destroying your nervous system, particularly slowing your respiration – as opposed to hemotoxic venom, which causes intense pain near the bite. The two venomous snakes known to be found in the Gobi possess a primarily hemotoxic venom.

- Melts someone's skin? Certain venom will do this. A hemotoxic or cytotoxic venom will melt through flesh, and even bone. If it's a spitting snake the venom can cause blindness, and, I can tell you from experience, it burns when you get it on your skin. I can see where it would be confused for acid, blood, or poison.

- Spits hot acid, venom, blood, or poison? I'd be more likely to believe there was a spitting snake in Mongolia than a death worm.

- Lives in the area? The geographically closest known spitting-snake species is the mangshan pitviper in China. Note: there are eight species of snakes in Mongolia. Two are vipers and five are elapids. All known "spitting" snakes are elapids or vipers. The eighth species is a sand boa, which most closely resembles the physical descriptions of a death worm.

Could the death worm be all of the snake species of the Gobi getting combined into one story? Could it have the appearance of a sand boa but the behaviors of a spitting viper or elapid? Or a new, undescribed, species of snake? It's possible. Likely even, I'd say. I think it's most likely a known or unknown snake species with its behaviors and characteristics exaggerated to the point of seeming absurd.

A lizard like an amphisbaena, sandfish (Scincus scincus), or horned lizard

- Color? Check – particularly some amphisbaenas.
- Size? Check.
- Shape? Check – the shape of an amphisbaena (squatter and fatter than most snakes) works even better than a snake, in fact.
- "Head and tail look the same"? Check – actually, the name "amphisbaena" comes from a mythical Greek creature with a head on either end of its body.
- Burrowing? Check – moves forward and backward with ease in a bizarre movement where the skin drags the body along, and the skin is loosely connected. My personal experience with them leads me to think that their bizarre locomotion – much different than a snake – would tend to make people think some pretty bizarre things about them. They seem to hover over the earth and move with a disconcerting, unearthly grace, like they aren't actually exerting any effort. Likewise, I could see the sandfish's movement leading to some tall tales. As its name implies, it seems to swim through the sand.

- Electric? No, but same argument as above.
- Exploding? Maybe – same argument as above.
- Touching it can cause death? No.
- Spits hot acid, venom, blood, or poison? Yes, the horned lizard shoots blood out of its eyes.
- Melts someone's skin? No, but there are venomous lizards. The most famous being the Gila monster, which lives in the North American deserts and bears a passing resemblance to the death worm.
- Lives in the area? There are a few known lizard species in the Gobi, and at one point in history there was an amphisbaena.
  - There is a case to be made for a living fossil or a possible out-of-place species that has popped up in a new location out of its natural range, and either established a breeding population (as in the Burmese pythons in the Florida Everglades), or simply lives out its probably short life, frightening any locals who happen upon it (as in alligators in New England, which turn up every summer). These possibilities are easier to swallow than an entirely unique phylum of creatures shooting lightning bolts out of their mouths. In a fairly isolated part of the world that relies heavily on oral tradition, has a rich storytelling history, and associates extraordinary abilities with known, harmless animals, sightings of such odd, out-of-place or extremely rare survivors wouldn't have to happen frequently to create a legend and help it thrive.

Yes, I'd have to say the death worm could be a lizard – either misidentification of a known one or potentially a new lizard species.

A true worm

Amazingly, and seemingly going against what science had been saying for years, in 2012 two species of earthworm were named in Mongolia. It was thought that the Gobi was too dry and the temperature varied too greatly for an earthworm to survive. Once again, science was wrong. It's mind-blowing to me that this wasn't a bigger story in the crypto communities. It's no surprise that it was buried in scientific literature, and no mainstream news sources would be expected to pick it up – they are earthworms after all – but crypto-blogs should have been all over this! In more exciting worm news (not a statement you hear every day, but I mean it sincerely), the largest species of earthworm in Britain was discovered in 2016, on a Scottish island. The big guy (actually all earthworms are hermaphrodites) is an impressive and emasculating 18 inches.

- Color? Check – worms come in a variety of colors.
- Size? Check – actually, some worms are huge. The bootlace worm is found on the coasts on Britain and reaches an astonishing 180 feet. Terrestrial species of earthworms can attain massive sizes as well. A species in Africa averages about seven feet, but one specimen was found in the 1960s that was a staggering 22 feet long. A species in Australia can reach over nine feet long, and America's longest wiggler is over three feet, rumored to smell of lilies and said to spit in self-defense. (That is not a joke – only some innuendos are intentional in this section.) The scent and spitting have not been observed in the very few specimens found in modern times, and only a handful have been located since the mid-1900s.
- Shape? Check – worms are, without a doubt, worm shaped.
- "Head and tail look the same"? Check – even worms can't tell which side is which when they first meet each other.

- Burrowing? Check – earthworms do, in fact, live in the earth.
- Electric? Nope.
- Exploding? Maybe – same argument as above.
- Touching it can cause death? No, but there are many species of worms that are toxic if eaten or are coated in toxic slime, while others carry deadly parasites. The Guinea flatworm has both. Its outer coating of slime will make you sick if you ingest it and it carries the rat-lung parasite – a wonderful-sounding little bugger that burrows into your brain.
- Spits hot acid, venom, blood, or poison? No, but it's weird that the giant Palouse Earthworm (America's largest) is also said to spit in self-defense.
- Melts someone's skin? No.
- Lives in the area? Would have said "no" before 2012, but now – check.

The main reason people think the death worm is a worm is the name, "Death Worm", but this is an imperfect translation. The Mongolian word describes the shape – meaning "like an intestinal worm" – rather than implying the creature *is* a worm. I will say that it is certainly not one of the known species of earthworm in Mongolia – they are too small and thin. There is the potential for a new species of worm though, as unlikely as that sounds.

The whole checklist thing gets pretty repetitive, so it's not happening anymore. Heads up.

Amphibian

Interestingly, there are five known species of amphibians in Mongolia. One is a tree frog. How bizarre is that? A tree frog in the Gobi Desert! That's what a strangely diverse place the Gobi is. One of the known species is the Siberian Salamander. Saying this guy is hardy would be like saying Boston got some snow in February 2015 (google it). These salamanders can survive being frozen in permafrost for years. When the temperatures finally rise enough they just sort of walk it off and continue with their clearly not very agenda-driven lives. There aren't many creatures who can just stop being alive for years, then pick right up where they left off. "Where was I going today/three years ago? Oh yeah, over to that rock to see if there are any slugs near it."

While I seriously doubt there is an amphibian than can electrocute you, there definitely are ones that can mess you up just from touching them. They aren't found in Mongolia, but many species of amphibians secrete toxins that can kill (poison dart frogs – some just from touching them, others from ingesting them), make you sick (cane toad), make you trip (Colorado River toad), or burn your skin (smoky jungle frog). I've caught all of these species and can tell you that the smoky jungle frog is seriously freaky. My friend from the *Nature Calls* crew actually caught it, and when it started screaming, he and I both screamed back:

"Pat, I just caught a huge weird-looking frog with red eyes! Check this thing out!" (Hands it to me.)

Frog: "AHHHHH!!"

Me: "AHHHHH! What the HELL IS HAPPENING?"

Frog: "Meep. AHHHHHHHH!!! AHHHHHHHHHH!!!"

Me: "This is so messed up! Holy shit, my hands are burning!"

Frog: "AHHHHHHHHHHHHHHHH!!!!"

It reportedly sounds like a cat. I've had cats my whole life – this sounded like a pissed-off infant. After holding it for a few seconds my hands started to burn. If the nomads made up stories about a harmless snake shooting through a camel because it moved fast, I can't imagine what they'd come up with if they came across anything like a smoky jungle frog.

I've also caught a Colorado River toad and, while I didn't partake of the psychoactive venom it secretes, it's supposed to be a powerful hallucinogen. Let's postulate that there is an amphibian in Mongolia secreting a psychotropic drug from its skin and a few nomads have touched it and tripped their faces off. Might they have "seen" an animal shooting blue lightning, exploding, melting their skin off, burning their faces, shooting blood, moving forward and backward at the same time, and generally acting nightmarish? Sounds like a pretty standard "bad trip" to me.

The defense strategy of blowing oneself up is called autothysis, from the Greek words for "self" and "sacrifice" – and is not much of a defense for the individual since it results in the animal's death, but, it can help a colony. This strategy is only seen in ants and termites (will be talked about in more depth later), but, plenty of animals suck in air or water to make themselves appear bigger or make themselves more difficult to swallow, and in the process, some get overenthusiastic and occasionally pop themselves. The Indian Balloon frog is famous for inflating itself to pufferfish-like proportions. Plenty of other frogs inflate their neck pouches to call mates, and most toads can suck in air to nearly double their size. In 2005, more than 1000 "exploded" toads were found in a pond in Hamburg, Germany. Some people even observed these animals explode after inflating to over three times their original size. The explosions are said to have sprayed toad-guts over three feet in every direction. One theory was that they were being predated with great frequency and felt so threatened that they were overinflating themselves and bursting like balloons, others said that local crows had developed a taste for toad livers and had already removed these with surgical-like precision prior to the explosions. The next time the toads tried their natural inflation defense, the hole from the liver removal caused a malfunction-overinflation and left the body weakened, which led to guts flying. While this was an extreme number of cases, it's not unusual to find "popped" frogs and toads – no crow-surgeons necessary.

I'd be confident in saying it's entirely possible that the Mongolian Death Worm is some type of amphibian.

An unknown insect

This was initially proposed by our episode producer after seeing our guides' hesitance to touch the grubs I had dug up. He started asking me what the largest grub was. I replied that my guess was that it would be that of the goliath beetles. I was wrong. We don't actually know what the largest grub is because we've never found the larvae of a titan beetle (debatably the largest beetle on Earth), but boreholes in wood leave entomologists guessing that it might be a foot long and a couple inches wide. There are a few grubs that we know of that are over six inches long and fat – the stuff of nightmares if you suffer from entomophobia. These grubs would all classify as the right size and shape for the death worm.

A knock against this idea is that all of them live in moist rotting wood, which is not found in the Gobi. However, many grub species live underground, including the ones I dug up. Another knock against this idea is that a giant grub generally leads to a giant beetle or moth, of which we have no reports from the Gobi. Some possible explanations for our lack of a giant winged insect are as follows:

- Maybe the beetle also lives underground.
- Maybe the moth or beetle is so short lived that it's never been found. Many grubs stay grubs for years, like cicadas (16+ years) and the giants mentioned above, and some only live as an adult for a few days. This could be the case here, where you are more likely to see the grub than the adult insect, and very unlikely to see either.
- Maybe the migration as an adult takes it far from the

Gobi, like Monarchs traveling to Mexico? This is a big stretch, however, I'll admit.

In regards to some of the MDW's defenses, besides the aforementioned bombardier beetles, there are also a group of about 15 species of ants in Southeast Asia that blow themselves up in order to fend off predators trying to attack the colony. These so-called "exploding ants" are filled with toxic chemicals and contract a part of their abdomen called a gaster so tightly that their bodies rupture and this stinky, sticky, toxic goo sprays outward at everything close by – immobilizing and killing any would-be colony-destroying attackers. Sounds pretty death-worm-ish to me.

While the insect hypothesis checks some boxes – size, shape, color, crunches when you step on it, bites if you poke it, explodes, etc. – it's a harder sell than a snake, lizard, or even worm. The only scenario that makes this believable is a grub, and only if the adult beetle is fossorial as well.

Summation

So, where does this leave us? Unfortunately, not in great place. I think I've shown that it is very unlikely that there is any animal in the Gobi Desert with all the traits and powers the Mongolian Death Worm is said to possess. I think I've also shown that the Nomads of Mongolia do not actively seek out animals when they don't need to, and don't mess with ones they happen to come across. They also make up elaborate stories about known animals based on their limited interactions with them and a lot about the death worm has an air of "the moral of this story is mind your own goddam business when dealing with any form of life in the Gobi" – a good rule to live by, in all fairness, and not just in the Gobi.

I've also shown quite a few animals who do, in reality, possess some of the traits of the death worm, and pointed to some animals who could be confused for the death worm or could have started the legends about it. There is also the fairly high potential that there is an unknown animal in the Gobi exhibiting at least some of the traits of the death worm, and this is what I tend to lean towards.

I believe it is entirely possible that there is a new species of burrowing animal in the Gobi and that it has inspired the stories about the death worm. I believe it may even possess some of the "powers" of the death worm. Maybe it spits venom or blood, maybe it just looks like it *could* spit by the way it moves, maybe it makes a weird noise, maybe touching it makes your hand burn, maybe it makes you hallucinate, maybe it actually is somewhat dangerous, maybe, maybe, maybe... the truth is, we just don't know. Based on what we see in other creatures, I doubt very much there is an animal that actually behaves as the death worm is said to. But worms, amphibians, reptiles, and insects have been found pretty recently in the Gobi Desert, so who's to say there aren't more species left to find? And although the death worm is most likely just a sand boa with the nomads putting their unique twist on it, Harry was right, maybe there really is *something* to the legend. Who am I to say? I only spent a couple weeks there, and was drunk for a fair portion of it.

Acknowledgements

While I have dedicated this book to Anna, Luna, and Wally (my father was quick to point out the inappropriateness of this, noting some of the adult content and the fact that the kids won't be able to read it for a few years), I truly could not have completed it without the help of the many incredible people I am so fortunate to have in my life. I'd like to take a minute to thank each of them.

A bit more on Anna – my phenomenal wife. She not only joins me on many adventures, but has put up with all of the insanity that comes with being a partner to a guy who does all of the stuff described in here.

And our kids, Luna Caulfield and Wallace Charles. The greatest aspect of my life is being a part of theirs.

My insane and wonderful family – Al, Mom, Sarah, and Nathan who have supported and encouraged me throughout my life. Mom, who learned more about alligator reproduction than she probably ever wanted to in her quest to support a budding young biologist and Al who took me camping and fishing despite having no interest in these activities himself, which I never knew until I was in my late twenties. Sorry about child welfare having to come to the house and watch you change diapers and question Sarah about possible neglect/abuse after I got salmonella from a lizard, then spread it to about a dozen friends, and cracked my head open sledding, and sliced my legs open sliding down a hill to catch a snake – hopefully this makes up for the embarrassment?

The entire current and past Icon family, particularly Harry

and Laura Marshall. Harry and Laura are two of my favorite people on Earth. They are the people Anna and I want to be when we grow up. They are the smartest, nicest, funniest, and most caring and loving people you could hope to meet, and the greatest thing about doing TV has been having them enter our lives. We love them like family. In addition to Harry and Laura there's Andie Clare, Lucy Middleboe, Stephen McQuillan, Barny Revill, James Bickersteth, Alex Holden, Anna Gol, Ben Roy, Laura Coates, Sol Welch, Belinda Partridge, Abi Wrigley, Duncan Fairs, Robin Cox, Simon Reay, Rupert Miles, Brendan McGinty, and everyone else, who continue to be amazing forces of encouragement and support.

The Nat Geo team behind *Beast Hunter* – Janet Han Vissering, Steve Burns, Ashley Hoppin, Sydney Suissa, Russel Howard, Chris Albert, Geoff Daniels, Mike Mavretic, Dara Klatt, Steve Ashworth, Whit Higgins, and others. Thank you so much for your support and trust in allowing me to fulfill a lifelong dream, and letting Icon take the lead and make a series we are all really proud of.

The most amazing and supportive group of friends I could ask for – Adam Manning, Dom Pellegrino, Joe Viola, and Adrianna Wooden. Thank you for sticking by me and being there for me and my family through everything.

Thank you so much to the entire team at John Hunt Publishing, especially John Hunt, who saw the potential of the massive and messy manuscript I sent over, Dominic James, who assured all of my insecurities and answered all of my question while reassuring me that it was all going to be okay, and the expert editing of Graham Clarke, who managed to pull these six books together and make them the cohesive series.

Acknowledgements

My very literary friends and family who served as the first reviewers of this book – Al Spain, Joe Viola, Dom Pellegrino, Richard Sugg, Sarah Franchi, Gene Campbell, Tim Fogarty, John Johnson, Zeb Schobernd, Sarahbeth Golden, and Luke Kirkland – thank you for your insights and mocking. This book is much better because of you.

The folks at my day job who have supported my insane extracurricular activities – especially Bill O'Connor who gave me the opportunity to do this and assured me I'd still have a job when I returned.

Thanks to all of the incredible fixers, guides, and translators who kept us alive and safe, often risking your own lives in the process.

Thanks, finally, to the readers and fans of these shows! I hope you've enjoyed what you've seen and read! You can find all of my social media stuff at www.patspain.com. I try to answer questions and respond as best I can. Genuinely – thank you!

Continue the adventure with the Pat Spain On the Hunt Series

A Little Bigfoot: On the Hunt in Sumatra
Pat Spain lost a layer of skin, pulled leeches off his neither regions and was violated by an Orangutan for this book
Paperback: 978-1-78904-605-2
ebook: 978-1-78904-606-9

200,000 Snakes: On the Hunt in Manitoba
Pat Spain got and lost his dream job, survived stage 3 cancer, and laid down in a pit of 200,000 snakes for this book.
Paperback: 978-1-78904-648-9
ebook: 978-1-78904-649-6

A Living Dinosaur: On the Hunt in West Africa
Pat Spain was nearly thrown in a Cameroonian prison, learned to use a long-drop toilet while a village of pygmy children watched, and was deemed "too dirty to fly" for this book.
Paperback: 978-1-78904-656-4
ebook: 978-1-78904-657-1

A Bulletproof Ground Sloth: On the Hunt in Brazil
Pat Spain participated in the most extreme tribal ritual, accidentally smuggled weapons, and almost lost his mind in the Amazonian rainforest for this book.
Paperback: 978-1-78904-652-6
ebook: 978-1-78904-653-3

The Mongolian Death Worm: On the Hunt in the Gobi Desert
Pat Spain ingested toxic "foods", made a name for himself in traditional Mongolian wrestling, and experienced the worst bathroom on Earth for this book.
Paperback: 978-1-78904-650-2
ebook: 978-1-78904-651-9

Sea Serpents: On the Hunt in British Columbia
Pat Spain went to the bottom of the ocean, triggered a bunch of
very angry fisherman, and attempted to recreate an iconic scene
from Apocalypse Now for this book.

Paperback: 978-1-78904-654-0
ebook: 978-1-78904-655-7

Recent bestsellers from 6th Books are:

The Afterlife Unveiled
What the Dead Are Telling us About Their World!
Stafford Betty
What happens after we die? Spirits speaking through mediums
know, and they want us to know. This book unveils their world...
Paperback: 978-1-84694-496-3 ebook: 978-1-84694-926-5

Spirit Release
Sue Allen
A guide to psychic attack, curses, witchcraft, spirit attachment,
possession, soul retrieval, haunting, deliverance, exorcism and
more, as taught at the College of Psychic Studies.
Paperback: 978-1-84694-033-0 ebook: 978-1-84694-651-6

I'm Still With You
True Stories of Healing Grief Through Spirit Communication
Carole J. Obley
A series of after-death spirit communications which uplift, comfort
and heal, and show how love helps us grieve.
Paperback: 978-1-84694-107-8 ebook: 978-1-84694-639-4

Less Incomplete
A Guide to Experiencing the Human Condition Beyond the
Physical Body
Sandie Gustus
Based on 40 years of scientific research, this book is a dynamic
guide to understanding life beyond the physical body.
Paperback: 978-1-84694-351-5 ebook: 978-1-84694-892-3

Advanced Psychic Development
Becky Walsh
Learn how to practise as a professional, contemporary spiritual medium.
Paperback: 978-1-84694-062-0 ebook: 978-1-78099-941-8

Astral Projection Made Easy
and overcoming the fear of death
Stephanie June Sorrell
From the popular Made Easy series, *Astral Projection Made Easy* helps to eliminate the fear of death, through discussion of life beyond the physical body.
Paperback: 978-1-84694-611-0 ebook: 978-1-78099-225-9

The Miracle Workers Handbook
Seven Levels of Power and Manifestation of the Virgin Mary
Sherrie Dillard
Learn how to invoke the Virgin Mary's presence, communicate with her, receive her grace and miracles and become a miracle worker.
Paperback: 978-1-84694-920-3 ebook: 978-1-84694-921-0

Divine Guidance
The Answers You Need to Make Miracles
Stephanie J. King
Ask any question and the answer will be presented, like a direct line to higher realms… *Divine Guidance* helps you to regain control over your own journey through life.
Paperback: 978-1-78099-794-0 ebook: 978-1-78099-793-3

The End of Death
How Near-Death Experiences Prove the Afterlife
Admir Serrano
A compelling examination of the phenomena of Near-Death
Experiences.
Paperback: 978-1-78279-233-8 ebook: 978-1-78279-232-1

Where After
Mariel Forde Clarke
A journey that will compel readers to view life after death in a
completely different way.
Paperback: 978-1-78904-617-5 ebook: 978-1-78904-618-2

Harvest: The True Story of Alien Abduction
G L Davies
G. L. Davies's most terrifying investigation yet reveals one
woman's terrifying ordeal of alien visitation, nightmarish visions
and a prophecy of destruction on a scale never before seen in
Pembrokeshire's peaceful history.
Paperback: 978-1-78904-385-3 ebook: 978-1-78904-386-0

The Scars of Eden
Paul Wallis
How do we distinguish between our ancestors' ideas of God and
close encounters of an extra-terrestrial kind?
Paperback: 978-1-78904-852-0 ebook: 978-1-78904-853-7

Readers of ebooks can buy or view any of these bestsellers by clicking on the live link in the title. Most titles are published in paperback and as an ebook. Paperbacks are available in traditional bookshops. Both print and ebook formats are available online.

Find more titles and sign up to our readers' newsletter at http://www.johnhuntpublishing.com/mind-body-spirit.

Follow us on Facebook at https://www.facebook.com/OBooks and Twitter at https://twitter.com/obooks.